How To S
in College and U
Specific Learnir

HUMAN HORIZONS SERIES

How To Succeed in College and University with Specific Learning Difficulties

#Autism Spectrum Conditions
#Dyslexia #Dyspraxia #DCD #ADHD #Dyscalculia
#Language and communication disorders

A Guide for Students, Educators & Parents

Amanda Kirby

A Condor Book
Souvenir Press (E&A) Ltd

First published in Great Britain in 2013 by Souvenir Press Ltd.,
43 Great Russell Street, London WC1B 3PD

ISBN 978-0-28564-243-0

Typeset by M Rules

Printed and bound by CPI Group (UK) Ltd, Croydon, CR0 4YY

Contents

How To Succeed
in College and University with
Specific Learning Difficulties

Acknowledgements

Writing this book has only been possible because of the contribution of the many students who have told me their experiences of going to college and university. Their tales have helped me to understand some of the challenges and also how they have found ways to be successful and what has worked for them.

Additionally, a big thank you to all the parents that have also contributed information over the years to understand what it is like for them as well, their concerns, their challenges, and their tips for success, in supporting their children when making the move to further and higher education.

Finally, to the whole team at The Dyscovery Centre at University of Wales, South Wales, to Leyna Rees and most of all to Lynne Peters, thanks to all who have worked so hard to help put this book together.

I also have to thank my long suffering family for putting up with me!

Introduction

Moving from school to a new learning environment, whether university or college, can feel like a steep learning curve for most students, but for some, adapting to university or college life can seem much more of a challenge.

College life can seem a big jump from the school you may have attended for the last five years, and may require a new set of skills and certainly will provide many new experiences. As a student you may have walked to a local school and now need to use public transport for example. You will meet many new students of all ages, and may have left behind old friends and acquaintances. You will be starting a new course, perhaps in a completely new area of knowledge and have little understanding of what is expected in terms of outcomes for yourself or by others.

College and university approaches to teaching may be very different from the classroom based approaches you are used to with 25-30 students in a class and being in a familiar setting. Teaching may now be carried out in much larger groups or lecture style, or alternatively you may be expected to do more work alone or working in small groups.These new ways of working may mean you have to be able to quickly adapt to the other students' ways of working and to meet their as well as your expectations. No longer will a teacher chase you if you don't meet a deadline as you will be expected to remember where you need to be and what you need to do.

University life may also mean moving from the family home to a hall of residence, or alternatively living with fellow students in a flat. This will result in a social setting with potentially completely new sets of rules. It often means needing instantly to have the skills to shop and cook for meals for yourself and/or with others (not surviving on the local chip shop alone!). You will need to be prepared to make choices over your spending and budget. You now have the opportunity to decide what and where to be at any time and do this all without parental guidance or supervision (unless you remain at home, where there may still be some limits to the way you behave).

For most students this is an exciting time, but for some it may provoke anxiety, feeling uncertain whether they can cope with all the changes that could happen. Some may feel they have not had enough life experiences before going to university or college to be ready to make every decision and feel they still need someone around to be able to consider the rights and wrongs. In some cases living at home and having parental support can mean that university or college can be experienced successfully and there remains a safety net (i.e. support from others e.g. parents).

As a student, there is an expectation from the

college or university that you are ready (pretty much) to be able to organise most aspects of your life, including course work, home and social life. Unsurprisingly, having to juggle all of these different things may leave some students uncertain whether they can keep 'all the plates spinning' i.e. manage multiple tasks *and* cope with all of them.

Some students with Specific Learning Difficulties because of challenges going through school may have had less experience socialising and mixing with a variety of people. This may be for a number of reasons such as it was harder for you to make and keep friends, you have had poor experiences with your peers such as being bullied; or maybe because you prefer not being with larger groups your own age, and prefer older people's company such as your parent's or guardian's friends.

However, if you can identify early what the challenges are likely to be for you and try out some of the strategies, then you have a much greater chance of success both socially and educationally. It is so much better to be prepared and ready to go, than wait till problems start arising and you are having to deal with these, along with other demands, which can then cause you even potentially greater stress.

This book is therefore designed to help overcome these challenges by providing a wide range of helpful information, easy to use advice and sign posting to a wide range of resources that aim to prepare you for all aspects of university and college life.

You can approach reading this book in a number of ways:

- You can just look up a website or link to a useful app. There are hundreds of links to well tested ideas and tools to help you.
- You can read through a specific chapter on a topic area.
- You can read it from start to finish in chronological order.

It is intended to be a quick and easy to use, practical guide.

It has been written mainly to address issues specific to college and university but does also include information on coping with day to day living and managing a new and potentially changing social life.

Who is this book for?

This book is aimed at students with Specific Learning Difficulties and their parents/guardians.

Additionally, student support services and schools preparing students for the next steps may also find it helpful.

The book has been written with a particular focus on those individuals who may have any one (or more) of the following diagnoses or for those who think they may one of these conditions.

Some students may also have similar challenges but without a formal 'label'.

- Autism Spectrum Disorder (ASD) (also including Asperger's Syndrome)
- Attention Deficit Hyperactivity Disorder (ADHD) (also including ADD)
- Dyscalculia
- Dyslexia
- Dyspraxia (also known as Developmental Co-ordination Disorder/DCD)
- Specific Language Impairments

The way the guidance is given throughout the book and the tips and hints have been written with particular reference to you as a student, who has one or more Specific Learning Difficulty to a lesser or greater degree. It aims to highlight where challenges may lie, and then to provide tips and hints to help you to succeed based on other students' experiences and from research evidence.

The style of the content of the book also considers some of these challenges that you may have in particular if you are the reader. For example, some people with Autism Spectrum Disorder may find they sometimes take things literally, and so explanations may be given for phrases used to assist with understanding and make it clear what is meant.

Some of you may have Dyslexia type difficulties and so may find reading texts harder to do, and this is one of the reasons for providing this book as an electronic book so it can be listened to as an alternative option.

NB. All the ideas in this book are also useful for any student starting out at college or university, but have been particularly considered for students with the above range of Specific Learning Difficulties.

CHAPTER 1

What are Specific Learning Difficulties?

This chapter outlines what Specific Learning Difficulties (SpLD) are and the challenges in college and university that may present to you and to others. This information may also be helpful for you to use to discuss with fellow students, lecturers and student services if they are unfamiliar with the pattern and type of Specific Learning Difficulty you may have and how it impacts on your life.

What's in a label?

Different terms have been used to describe the overall umbrella of different challenges.

Terms such as:

- Specific Learning Difficulties
- Hidden impairments
- Developmental disorders
- Learning disabilities
- Learning difficulties
- Neurodiversity
- Neurodevelopmental disorders

Different professionals use these terms in different ways, often causing some confusion. For example, in America, Learning Disabilities is often used as a term to mean reading difficulties, whereas in the UK it usually refers to individuals with intellectual disabilities i.e. of lower intellectual ability. Some people don't like the terms disorder, impairment or disability and prefer the term condition. Other people prefer to describe to others their challenges (and their strengths) and avoid 'labelling' themselves. Some students prefer to see themselves as neurodiverse and not disabled at all, but just different to others and the world potentially disabling them. This is more a social model rather than a medical model where the health or educational professional provides you with a 'label' or diagnosis.

Being neurodiverse has its benefits in the way you see the world. It can be thought by some that it is society and their views and approaches which disable you rather than the other way around. If people only understood and recognised the strengths as well as the challenges they would see Specific Learning Difficulties as a potentially different and exciting way to see the world.

- How do you describe yourself to others?
- Do you talk about your diagnosis?
- Do you first describe your strengths?
- You are you ... and you have a diagnosis – the label is not who you are!
- Do you see yourself as dyslexic for example or someone with Dyslexia?

The diagnosis

In school or in early life you may have been given a diagnosis.

The diagnosis you got (or didn't) may be dependent on varying factors:

- Which professional you were seen by as a child or teenager (and what skills they have or had at that time)
  - Some professionals may have greater knowledge and understanding of some Specific Learning Difficulties than others.
  - Your GP or teacher may not know/have known much about one condition and so may have sent you to a specialist in a field they knew more about e.g. recognising the signs and symptoms of Dyslexia, but not know much about ADHD or ASD. They may have referred you where there were services or a shorter waiting list. In many parts of the country there are no clinics for ADHD in adulthood hence it is easier to get a diagnosis of Dyslexia than ADHD despite you potentially having this diagnosis.
- What assessments have been undertaken (or what has not been assessed!)
  - This may be dependent on what the professional has been trained to use.
  - How much time they have to assess you e.g. assessments for ASD can take several hours to complete.
  - What assessment kit they have available.

Some assessments cost over £1000 to
purchase and so they may not have them
because of the cost.

- Why you have gone to them. Some
  assessments are undertaken to provide a
  specific report for additional equipment
  or support. This means the assessment is
  undertaken to provide information in a
  specific format.

- How old you are
  - It is likely that if you are an adult over 35
    years of age, you are more likely to have
    been given a diagnosis of Dyslexia, than one
    of Dyspraxia or ADHD, as you would have
    been less likely to have been diagnosed while
    in childhood as less was known about these
    conditions 20 years ago. If you had a
    diagnosis of DCD then you are likely have
    been given this in the last 10–15 years as
    terminology has changed.
  - The terms are changing again and with a new
    classification system from America, the term
    Asperger's has now been taken out of the
    terms being used by professionals. This leads
    to confusion in telling others what you have
    and what you don't!

- How you present your problems or challenges –
  this may mean that a professional looks more
  at one aspect than another
  - Depending on the pattern of your strengths
    and difficulties, this will make it more or less
    obvious to others what your diagnosis is. If

you have some challenges to a lesser degree in many areas, the result may be greater difficulty for you, but make it harder for someone else to 'label you' e.g. if most of your difficulties are around reading and spelling it will mean the professional will consider Dyslexia; if it is around social and communication challenges then they may consider speech and language difficulties or ASD.

- Where you live
  - Services vary still in many areas, especially for adolescents and adults. This may be dependent on local funding, or a specialist with a particular interest. This is especially true for adults who may want an assessment for ADHD or ASD. Many areas of the country lack services at all and it can be just luck if your GP knows where to send you.

An overlapping picture

Most students coming to college or university if they already have a diagnosis of a Specific Learning Difficulty will tend to have been given one 'label' or diagnosis. However, it is important to recognise that despite you possibly having one diagnosis, condition, or disorder (terms other people use) in reality the evidence shows that most individuals usually do not have challenges in just one specific area. We are a mixture of both our genetics and our environment, in fact both have interactive influences on us. Secondly, those that have a neurodiverse brain may have a pattern of difficulties and strengths that are unique to them. Your brain does not neatly separate out the different areas of functioning and work in isolation and so this is not a surprising reality.

In fact, there is lots of research evidence to show that an individual with only one area of isolated difficulty is actually quite unusual. For example, someone with Dyslexia will often have some level of attention and concentration difficulties as well (in around 25–40% of cases) and someone with DCD/Dyspraxia may also often have challenges with organisation and attention and may find it harder to socialise with others. Planning what you do and doing something are often linked together, and so cannot in reality be separated into artificial boxes. Dyscalculia (maths difficulties) often also overlaps with Dyslexia and DCD. Individuals with ASD often have some symptoms of ADHD and may have more co-ordination challenges.

For some people the reasons these are associated with each other, e.g. having a lack of opportunity to socialise with others, may impact on their actions. For example, someone with challenges in their motor skills may have avoided playing sport. This results in less opportunity to hang out with children of a similar age knocking a ball around in the playground or after school. This leads to less chance of chatting to others of a similar age and forging friendships. In time this results in you being more isolated and having less confidence, and social skills become less polished and practised than your peers.

Each student has their own unique pattern of strengths and challenges (like everyone else we cannot be easily described by a single label). Who you are today may also be related to your past experiences both good and bad (such as in school). Your confidence and self esteem may affect the way you present yourself to others, such as if you have been bullied or felt more isolated in your teen years.

Also, your experiences of being in a school and having access to a variety of different sports and having choices may have allowed you to find one you enjoyed and you continue to do so now such as swimming. In contrast, a school that only had football and netball as sporting choices, may have meant if you had co-ordination difficulties, that sports lessons filled you with a feeling of dread every week and this has stayed with you to today and you still avoid participating in any sports.

Additionally, the support you have received from others at home or school may have made a big difference to the way you are today. Your parents may have encouraged you to listen to books to overcome some reading difficulties for example, so you still gained knowledge despite your challenges, or a teacher may have allowed you to type in exams so you could show them your true ability. In contrast to this, your experience may have been a teacher who thought you were lazy and couldn't be bothered, or said 'if only you could focus on your work you would be so much more able'.

The diagnostic labels professionals often use represent a shortcut descriptor to understand approximately where areas of difficulties may be, but also can be a way of presenting some of your strengths if described appropriately. However, the downside of the label may be that some people have a preconceived view of you or your label based on their experiences of others, or what they have read in the broadsheets.

Understanding what areas may be challenging for you is important in order to consider ways to avoid or adapt to different situations and to show you at your best. But, also seeing who you are and your skills and motivations, and what you can do is essential.

Your challenges only present one small part of who you are. It is important to be able to discuss with others in a positive manner your approaches to finding ways past barriers you have found in your everyday life.

Sadly, at the present time 'the system' for support remains dependent on assessing and mapping out the student's difficulties first in order to gain support and far less time is taken on presenting strengths as a USP (Unique Selling Point) to others. This latter approach may be a better model for the future to help you consider where you want to be employed for example.

Considering both interests and motivations are essential to finding the best course to study and also the right college or university. For example, if you don't like making presentations and talking in public, choosing a course where this approach is used for many assignments probably wouldn't be a good choice for you. If a course requires you to do many work placements for short periods of time, and you find going into new and unfamiliar settings hard for you, then this type of course should generally be avoided. If you learn best by seeing and doing a task, then a practical based course would best suit you.

Do think about what you like best or least and how and where you prefer to study. The more you understand yourself, the more likely you can put yourself on the right course, and in the right setting. If you are not sure ask others around you that you trust to see what they think.

Some people seem to believe that if you work very hard at the problems you can get better at them. This is true in some cases. However, moving to college and university is a big change for all, and the more you are in a setting working with your strengths (going with the flow), rather than trying to minimise your challenges (going against the grain) the easier it will be for you and the more confident you are likely to feel.

What are the likely challenges in college and university?

Some individuals may move from secondary school to further education or employment either with or without a diagnosis.

However, everyone finds to some extent moving to a new environment will present new challenges as demands increase for them and they are required to be more independent.

Lack of experience

Some students, for example, may find that they have not had the opportunity to have been assessed or diagnosed with a specific area of learning difficulty in school days despite finding school days a challenge. Some may feel they have always struggled with one or more aspect of learning, for example, but not been sure why this was the case. At college or university they may have access to student support services for the first time and an opportunity to be assessed by an expert. Some individuals report that they only go for help at college or university because they hear a fellow student talk about the difficulties they have had and realise for the first time they are not alone.

For others, the way into support may come from a lecturer who sees both the potential and also the pattern of difficulties and then discusses this with you, giving you the encouragement to seek help from others.

Talking about yourself can seem scary to start with; not knowing what others will say or think. This can also feel very liberating but at the same time can make you feel anxious about what someone may say to you. You may have been encouraged to come forward for help because there have been a series of 'disasters' that have repeated themselves and have come to a head (i.e. someone has said you need to seek help otherwise you won't be able to make the best of yourself). This may have been something such as failing to turn up for an exam; using drugs that have reduced your ability to stay focused and ended up with being in trouble with police or falling out with friends and family and them pushing you forward (for your own good!).

Having your needs identified
Specific Learning Difficulties can present themselves in many different ways and differ greatly from one student to another; in many cases students can have traits of several learning difficulties at the same time and often have a mixture of difficulties. This is common. However the educational 'system' often makes it easier to obtain some 'labels' than others. The reason for this includes there being fewer professionals diagnosing some learning difficulties such as DCD/Dyspraxia and ADHD for example. This can be very frustrating for some students who have difficulties in more than one area e.g. in this case, having co-ordination difficulties as well as Dyslexia

for example, but not being diagnosed for the co-ordination difficulties.

This may present a challenge for you as a student obtaining an assessment as in some areas there may be fewer specialists with the skills required to make a formal diagnosis, which may leave you feeling frustrated. In order to gain support it may be necessary for you to have a diagnosis and this may also come at a cost in both money and time. In some cases you may need to pay to have the assessment and report prepared for you to obtain specific aids e.g. computer programs and supports such as, a mentor, a scribe (someone that writes notes for you) or support from student services.

Additional challenges may come from others, including fellow students and lecturers, having little knowledge about your condition and how it presents for you. Some may have fixed views as well, believing that ADHD doesn't exist and is just an excuse you are giving to explain why you not doing some work! Someone else may believe that everyone is pretending to have Dyslexia to get free resources! Alternatively, they may not recognise the way you communicate is not intentionally being rude or abrupt but this has happened because you have not understood instructions or what someone has asked you to do and you have tried to ask for help.

Your challenges may also impact on others. Living with other students and sharing a kitchen or bathroom can mean you have to be sensitive to their, as well as your, needs. If you don't clear up because you don't notice the mess you have made, then this can cause anger and frustration from others. This can be especially true when you say you will do better next time and then forget to do so.

In college or university your lecturer who sees you arrive late for lectures again and again (because you are not good perhaps at time management and setting an alarm to prompt you to get up in time) may think you are being lazy and can't be bothered. Understanding others' perspectives is important for you to have support, but also for others to know why you have acted in a certain way.

What can be very frustrating, and not seem logical to some people, is how your challenges can vary from day to day and time to time. Having an understanding of yourself makes it easier for you to explain and ask for appropriate help. Letting people know why you have these challenges and asking them to help you, where appropriate, can create a support structure for success. However, there is a fine balance between asking and relying on people to be there and the strategies in this book can assist you to be more self reliant and know when to ask for help.

Unpacking 'Specific Learning Difficulties' (SpLD)

This term Specific Learning Difficulties covers a number of conditions, and individuals may be described as having a diagnosis of any of the following.

Attention Deficit Hyperactivity Disorder (ADHD)

Difficulty with attention and concentration, impulsiveness, restlessness and organizational and planning difficulties

Autism Spectrum Disorders (ASD) and Asperger's Syndrome

Social and communication difficulties

Dyscalculia

Mathematics difficulties

Dyslexia

Reading, spelling, recording difficulties

Dyspraxia (also known as Developmental Co-ordination Disorder (DCD))

Co-ordination difficulties in everyday life such as writing, preparing meals, driving a car, playing team sports

Speech, language and communication disorders

Understanding and speaking and communicating appropriately and effectively and in context

In addition individuals who may have any one of these conditions may also have Tourette's

Syndrome, and some individuals may have other conditions such as epilepsy as well.

Research has shown that some students may also be at a greater risk of feeling anxious and/or depressed at particular times in their lives and it is helpful for you to be aware of this and watch out for signs (or those close to you such as parents to know the signs) so you know when to ask for help and guidance.

Below is a brief description of each of the terms commonly used:

Key challenges for individuals with ADHD:

- Organisational skills such as work organisation, getting around new places and making appropriate decisions
- Impulsivity may show as difficulties in knowing which place to be in at the correct time; answering out of turn in tutorials; taking unnecessary risks and only thinking of the consequences afterwards
- Poor concentration which shows as difficulty completing tasks or assignments, or spending time web surfing
- Drifting off in meetings or lectures or when undertaking a task
- Poor time management seen as difficulties completing tasks in time; getting to places on time, or answering all the questions in a given

time frame; understanding how much time a task will take to be finished

- Fidgety when having to sit for any length of time or feeling restless inside
- Lose interest in a task before the end has been completed
- Initiation difficulties – difficulty getting off the 'starting block' to get work completed, so instead, spending time doing anything else to avoid it

Key challenges for individuals with Autism Spectrum Disorder (ASD) and Asperger's Syndrome:

- May be more socially isolated due to a difficulty making and keeping friends
- Understanding social rules such as how to speak and act towards others; you may appear to others as awkward when meeting people, avoiding direct eye contact for example
- Coping with change and being adaptable and flexible in different social environments
- Feeling fidgety or anxious in a situation which is overstimulating e.g. too many people, too much sound
- Harder coping with different lecturers' teaching styles especially in a small group setting
- Misunderstanding what has been said and taking instructions literally
- Difficulties expressing yourself clearly to others in a way they can understand

- Coping in the workplace and knowing what to do without clear rules
- Taking things literally – you may appear overly honest, saying it how you see it
- May find noisy situations harder to manage such as in canteens
- May also have co-ordination difficulties

Key challenges for individuals with Dyscalculia:

- May have difficulties with the 'language of mathematics' i.e. undertaking problems that are not in 'just' number format e.g. where the problem is requiring you to extract information to understand what is required of you
- May not have a 'real feel' for numbers – harder to make quick estimates e.g. in cooking, decorating etc.
- May have difficulty understanding and/or remembering maths terminology e.g. signs
- May experience difficulty with other concepts related to maths e.g. telling the time, managing money, taking measurements
- Slower doing simple mathematical tasks than others e.g. working out change in a shop

Key challenges for individuals with Dyslexia:

- Taking notes down on paper in a meeting or lecture

- Planning and writing documents or assignments
- Missing out information when listening to instructions
- Spelling mistakes in written work e.g. missing words out, getting confused by words sounding similar such as 'reed' and 'read'
- Slower reading information and need to re-read it several times to gain the meaning
- Learning new vocabulary in the different topic areas
- May avoid reading out loud in a group setting
- Difficulty noticing spelling errors when proofing an assignment

Key challenges for individuals with DCD/Dyspraxia:

- Slower writing notes legibly in a lecture
- Difficulty for others reading their writing
- Organising self and activities – late with assignments, lose possessions
- Prioritising tasks
- Time concepts – late for meetings, or very early; difficulty knowing how long a task will take
- Using scissors and other equipment needing good motor control
- Driving and orienteering around new places
- Slower learning a new or less familiar skill
- Packing bags or filing notes may be harder to do

- Ironing and folding clothes
- Preparing hot meals from scratch and to time can be stressful
- Learning to drive, park and estimate distances

Key challenges for individuals with speech, language and communication disorders:

- Remembering a sequence of instructions
- Taking down telephone numbers or instructions
- Need to be shown rather than told, otherwise may make mistakes in tasks
- May appear anxious/angry as he/she does not understand what is being asked of him/her
- May appear shy or withdrawn
- May misunderstand what has been asked of him or her
- May have difficulty taking turns in meetings or tutorials
- May prefer to lead a group project rather than be led, so he/she will know what is going on
- Difficulty entering or leaving a conversation, especially in a group setting
- May have problems being understood by others – speech may be indistinct

If you feel that you (or someone you know) may have one or more of the specific learning difficulties listed, there are lots of organisations that can provide you with help and advice.

See the relevant organisations listed on page 201 onwards.

You are so much more than a 'label'

Knowing your strengths

While everyday challenges have been described by using labels or descriptors it is important to remember you are not the label. It only describes one part of you and you should not be defined by it. You are not, for example dyspraxic or dyslexic, but rather a person with Dyslexia or Dyspraxia.

It is essential to get to know what your strengths are.

- What do you like to do or would like to do, or did in the past and enjoyed very much?
- What are you passionate about?
- What do you or others consider your strengths to be?
- Are you:
  - a good listener
  - creative
  - precise
  - honest
  - exact
  - careful
  - musical
  - artistic
  - scientific
  - have good mechanical skills
  - have good IT skills
  - come up with new and interesting ideas
  - sociable
  - meticulous

- innovative
- logical
- caring
- empathic

Sometimes people with ASD find it hard to recognise in themselves their strengths. For others it may be because they have heard people describe their weaknesses all their lives. You may need to discuss with your parents, or someone who knows you well and cares about you, what they think are good words to describe you.

How have you overcome some of the barriers presented to you? Think of examples of what you have achieved over the years to get to college or university now. Are you hard working? Do you persevere despite the challenges? What hobbies and interests do you have that could be used to show others you have skills you could transfer into the workplace potentially when leaving college or university?

Have you been travelling abroad or in this country?

- This could show you as being independent and being able to make decisions on your own.

Have you helped out at a local football team?

- This could show you have good physical skills

Have you taken a computer apart and mended it?

- This could show you have good mechanical and logical skills and are persistent

Have you helped out in a local restaurant in the kitchen or at the table?

- This could show you have catering skills, or are sociable, and hard working

Have you done some voluntary work for a local scout or church group?

- This could show you have good team working skills, you are sociable, like working with children

Do you like making cakes or cooking?

- This could show you have creative skills and could use this as a potential area to develop

New beginnings

College and university offer you new opportunities to 'reinvent' yourself and be the person you want to be rather than the way others may have seen you in the past. (However, this does not mean lying about who you are or what you have done).

But we sometimes can all walk around with 'baggage' i.e. we keep telling others all about what we cannot do, and how it has always been and have a feeling that nothing can change. Leaving these thoughts behind, and seeing college or university as a new and fresh opportunity to plan for the future allows you to move forward into a new phase in your life.

Learn to use words to describe yourself in positive ways. Describe the things you have found to work with your challenges and the coping strategies you have developed – this shows others you have a measure of resilience and ingenuity. You can ask now for assistance as well if needed.

Disclosure at college and university

Disclosure is a term used to describe how you tell other people about some of the challenges you may have. This may feel difficult for many students and it may be hard to know when to tell friends, other students or lecturers about their difficulties at home or in college or university, or to do so at all.

Concern how others may view you may be a reason for not telling others that some things are harder for you in some settings. Everyone has their own set of strengths and difficulties and it is up to you when and if you tell others.

However, if you don't say anything there is a chance that they may misconstrue how you are and why you avoid certain situations, for example reading out loud in a group setting because this is hard for you to do; or being in a large group because you are not sure how to behave in this setting. This could be seen as being lazy, can't be bothered, or even antisocial.

Pros and Cons to consider

- By not disclosing it may be harder for you to get some help and for others to provide it for you. It is hard for student services to provide additional support if you don't say what you find problematic in the course for example
- Reasonable adjustments under the law cannot be made unless you tell others such as student support services
- You can choose to disclose when you apply to college or university (this allows help to be set up earlier) or once you have arrived
- You don't need to tell everyone you meet – you can decide who to talk to and who not to e.g. close friends and your lecturer but not all the other students
- You can ask for information to remain confidential between student services and your lecturers
- Telling friends may allow them to support you if there are problems occurring, but they may make 'funny' comments about you and with you. You need to be prepared also to be able to respond. This may be seen as friendly banter between friends and not targeted at you specifically.

See *useful addresses of specific organisations* that can give you more advice and information on your condition and also how to be supported, also go to *www.boxofideas.org* for additional websites.

CHAPTER 2

Preparing for College and University

This chapter is designed to give you all the help and advice you need about preparing for college and university.

It gives you some ideas how you may go about selecting a course or place to study.

If you are choosing to go to university, or study away from home, this chapter also discusses how best to plan for this.

Choosing your university/college

First, consider what you want to study.

- What are you interested in?
- Do you have a hobby that you enjoy and would like to take further?
- Have you shown any flair at school, or outside school?
- Is there a specific career you would like to work in or a sector of work such as retail, care, IT, building, science or teaching?

Many courses can be entered at a variety of levels, so if you do not think you have the qualifications then you may still be able to study by entering at a foundation level and building up your skills.

Leaving home or staying local

It is hard to decide at times whether to flee the nest or stay at home where you know the area. Sometimes this is a financial decision and you can't afford to go away, for others it may be because you are not sufficiently confident to do so.

If you have never been away from home for even a weekend without your family or friends it is likely you will find it very hard to suddenly leave. Think about how much support you need at the moment and if that went whether you would realistically still be able to cope.

When you leave home and go to college or university you need to be ready to be more self-organised. You will need to be able to juggle all sorts of things including managing finances, sorting out food, arranging social life, and sorting out work and deadlines much more than when you were at school.

Think about all of these factors when making a decision whether to go away from home or to stay nearby.

Discuss it with others close to you who know you if you are not so sure. You are better to succeed in small steps than to take a big leap and fall off the edge! (i.e. leave home and have to come back because it has not worked out).

Getting started

- **Go online** – each college or university will have a prospectus (a book containing information about the place and the courses they offer).
- Get the college or university prospectus and read through what they provide, the structure of the course and how the course is assessed.
- You may want courses that offer a range of options for assessment e.g. not being assessed only through written work, or just having an exam at the end or you providing a portfolio.
- You need to consider whether a course with continuous assessment processes is better than a mixture of examination and assessment.
  - Are you better at presenting your work than writing it – this may be true if writing and spelling are difficult for you?
  - Do you have difficulties getting across your ideas when presenting, so would prefer written work – this may be harder if communication skills are challenging for you?
  - Do you have difficulties sustaining project work and focusing on it – this may be true if you have difficulties with attention and concentration – you may prefer a fixed time exam?
  - Are you slower processing information e.g. you take a little longer to respond to questions when someone is talking to you,

and need additional time in an examination situation?

- **Find out about the student support** – what are the student support services like in the college or university you are considering?
  - Email them and ask them how they could support you.
  - Ask what they have they done to support other students with similar challenges in the past.
  - Think about what you might need in the way of support in college and write down some specific questions so you are prepared.
  - What did you find harder to do in school?
  - What help have you needed before?
  - What worked for you or who helped you?
  - What do you think would make a difference to you?

- **Make a list of areas you may need help with studying and at home**
  - If you are not certain, ask your teacher or a parent/guardian what they think as well.

- **Go to the college/university open day**
  - See what the institution you are interested in has to offer you.
  - You may want to experience what the journey feels like to the place.
  - Be practical and think about how long it will take you to travel from home. Could this

bother you in winter for example or if you are on your own? Do you have difficulty using public transport? Do you get lost easily when going to an unfamiliar setting?

– A campus all on one site may be easier to get around than a college or university with several campuses spread across a city, especially if you need to travel between them.

– A city university may be spread across several sites and different lectures may be scattered.

Choosing where you want to live

Do you want to live away from home in student accommodation or stay at home?

If you want to stay in student accommodation have a check to see:

- How are the rooms arranged?
- Are they in flats and you are all sharing a communal kitchen?
  - Do you think you will be good at sharing a fridge with others?
  - Does others leaving a mess irritate you?
  - Do you tend to be messy and may irritate others?
- Are they mixed gender or is there an option for separate accommodation for males and females – which would you prefer?

- Is there an area where you can meet up together/eat together? Could this be a way to make friends or would communal eating bother you?
- How far are the halls of residence from the university and the town centre?
- What support is available at the halls of residence for study support or practical guidance?
- Is there an option to choose self-catering or catered?
- Are you near to shops or an ATM to get food or money if you run out?
- Is there a bus/train station nearby for you to go into town/home?

If you need or want to flat share:

- Go and see the accommodation office in the college or university. They often have a noticeboard to post your details.
- If you choose a flat you will need to give a 'bond' to start with; this is usually a month's rent, plus one month in advance. It could be useful to look on 'Gumtree' (*www.gumtree.com*) or an equivalent accommodation website, where there may be adverts locally. Many colleges and universities have a local bulletin board on the intranet or an accommodation office.
- Think about who to share with and how you match with their interests and the way you like

to live. Do you like partying and drinking late into the night or do you prefer quiet and early nights?

- Are you very tidy and organised? Are you someone that needs guidance to know what to do and when?

What amenities are close to your accommodation?

- Getting settled means finding out what facilities are around you. If you are new to the place then find out what's close to you e.g. gym, local shops for food supplies; nearest ATM to get money, somewhere to do some exercise, bus stop.
- If you feel very nervous thinking about all these changes it is often normal for most students starting off, but if it is bothering you a great deal then it may be a reason for staying closer to home and where you know your home environment.

Would a car be useful where you are going?

- If you need to use public transport, check on the access to this and availability. Find out what buses/trains allow you to travel from where you live to the college or university and how often they run. How much does this cost?
- Try and find out whether there is a university/

college bus service which is subsidised for students.

- Is the place you are going to difficult for you to travel to and you may need to have a car? Are you able to learn to drive or is this a challenge for you?
- Is car parking available for you?

Going home?

- What are the road/rail/bus links like and how much does it cost to get home?
- If it is more than a couple of hours away this may limit the frequency at which you can return. If you do need some extra support from home, it may be expensive for you to go back and forth, so a local university or college may be a better choice.

Do you prefer to stay at home?

If you stay at home – how far do you want to travel?

- If you still need support from your parents/guardians on a regular basis then you may want to consider being closer to home, living at home or remaining in your home town.
- If you have never lived away from home or been away on a holiday without your parents or close family, then moving away may be a big step for you. Staying at home also has

advantages, as it will mean that you are likely to already know the local landmarks such as the pubs, clubs and shops. You are probably more familiar with transport choices. You also have parents/guardians to provide some support (e.g. washing, shopping and ironing!)

Try to decide if you would prefer to go to a university in a city or a rural area

- Some campuses are based in the city, whereas others are in the countryside away from large towns – which do you prefer?

If you are still confused about whether you should move into student accommodation or live at home then use the chart on the next page to help you decide.

Moving to university/college – what should you take with you?

If you do decide to move to student accommodation whilst you are at university then you need to consider what you will or won't need to take with you in terms of your possessions, clothing etc.

There are probably many items you use at home that will not be available in halls of residence or a shared house so you will need to take them with you or buy new ones. However there is usually a limited space for everything, so don't try to take the whole house!

Moving to university/college

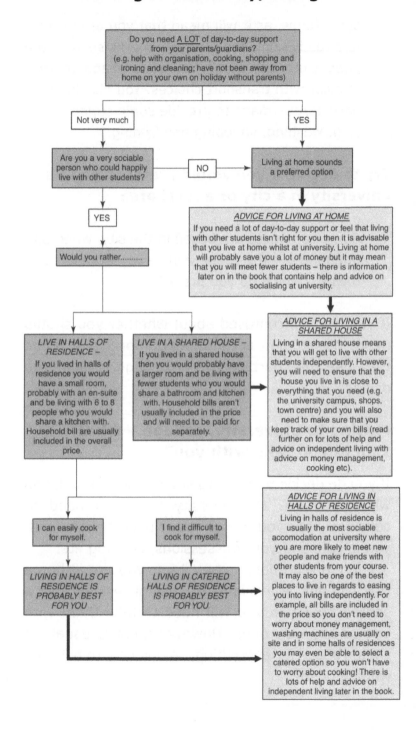

Do you need A LOT of day-to-day support from your parents/guardians? (e.g. help with organisation, cooking, shopping and ironing and cleaning; have not been away from home on your own on holiday without parents)

Not very much

YES

Are you a very sociable person who could happily live with other students?

NO

Living at home sounds a preferred option

YES

Would you rather..........

ADVICE FOR LIVING AT HOME

If you need a lot of day-to-day support or feel that living with other students isn't right for you then it is advisable that you live at home whilst at university. Living at home will probably save you a lot of money but it may mean that you will meet fewer students – there is information later on in the book that contains help and advice on socialising at university.

LIVE IN HALLS OF RESIDENCE –

If you lived in halls of residence you would have a small room, probably with an en-suite and be living with 6 to 8 people who you would share a kitchen with. Household bill are usually included in the overall price.

LIVE IN A SHARED HOUSE –

If you lived in a shared house then you would probably have a larger room and be living with fewer students who you would share a bathroom and kitchen with. Household bills aren't usually included in the price and will need to be paid for separately.

ADVICE FOR LIVING IN A SHARED HOUSE

Living in a shared house means that you will get to live with other students independently. However, you will need to ensure that the house you live in is close to everything that you need (e.g. the university campus, shops, town centre) and you will also need to make sure that you keep track of your own bills (read further on for lots of help and advice on independent living with advice on money management, cooking etc).

I can easily cook for myself.

I find it difficult to cook for myself.

LIVING IN HALLS OF RESIDENCE IS PROBABLY BEST FOR YOU

LIVING IN CATERED HALLS OF RESIDENCE IS PROBABLY BEST FOR YOU

ADVICE FOR LIVING IN HALLS OF RESIDENCE

Living in halls of residence is usually the most sociable accomodation at university where you are more likely to meet new people and make friends with other students from your course. It may also be one of the best places to live in regards to easing you into living independently. For example, all bills are included in the price so you don't need to worry about money management, washing machines are usually on site and in some halls of residences you may even be able to select a catered option so you won't have to worry about cooking! There is lots of help and advice on independent living later in the book.

Bedroom essentials

In student accommodation there is usually no bedding provided. Check and make sure what is actually provided. Some provide a duvet and pillows.

- You may need to take bed sheets, pillows and a duvet, towels and a spare set to change.
- There may also be other items you may want to take that aren't provided (e.g. desk lamp, kettle or mini fridge).
- Check the rules for your institution as there may be a limit on the number of electrical items that you can use and you may not be allowed to take some items such as a mini fridge.

Bathroom essentials

Don't forget to buy all your bathroom essentials e.g. toothpaste, toothbrush, shower gel, shampoo, shaver and toilet rolls.

- You should also take some cleaning products to use for the toilet and shower etc. if you have your own bathroom.
- Wipes can often be easier to use than anything else.
- Remember bin bags for personal 'rubbish' may also be required.

Kitchenware

Most student accommodation may have a microwave, toaster or kettle.

- You will probably need to take your own cutlery; plates, mugs and cooking utensils – a frying pan and saucepan are usually essential items. Don't spend too much on these as other students often use them as well!
- There may also be other electrical items that you wish to take that are not provided, like a blender, toasted sandwich maker or a coffee machine.

Other equipment to get started
Have a think what you need for your specific course.

Stationery
Most courses may require the following as basics:

- Pens and pencils
- Lever-arch files
- Box files
- Polypockets
- Folders – different colours for different course materials
- File dividers
- Staple gun and staples
- Hole puncher
- USB stick/external hard drive
- Sellotape, pair of scissors, paper clips, sticky labels

Personal items

If you are away from home also remember vital personal items:

- Mobile phone
- Purse/wallet
- Bank cards
- ID cards
- Photos for student cards
- Charger for phones and laptop etc.
- Laptop/notebook/notepad/portable printer/ tablet
- Pictures of family (if you want to)
- Passport if you are going on trips

Sit down and make a list of all the things that you will need to take with you when you move to university or college. Put this into your mobile phone so it is with you when you are shopping.

Start putting everything together in a box so you don't forget.

- Tick off items as you go along so you know that you have remembered everything.

Arriving at university

When you arrive at university there are lots of things you will need to consider, for example:

- Have you got your own bank account set up and ready to go, especially if you are away from home?
- If you are in a hall or flat, have you a 'starter pack' of food for the first few days?
- Have you paid your fees, or have registration forms etc. with you?
- Have you signed up with a doctor and a dentist?
- Do you know where to go to register and get your student card, keys etc. – there are usually people around that are allocated to help you. Go to the main entrance if you are not certain and ask there.

CHAPTER 3

Getting and Staying Organised

This chapter provides you with lots of help and advice that will help you with organising every aspect of college and university life, including your college/university life, your home life and your social life.

Organisational skills need to be practised and put in place for them to be remembered and used. Just waiting to be organised is not likely to happen and has to be a proactive activity.

In order to use your time efficiently and effectively you need to plan ahead and have routines in place. Start off by making sure your schedule is realistic. If you are not sure what to do and how to get organised ask others to help you that you can trust such as parents, student support services. Library services sometimes run study skills courses as well that may be of help. Student services can also be of help with your course work.

The following are some practical suggestions and strategies that many students have found useful and which may help you function more efficiently in university or college.

It does also help if you think about how to be organised *before* your move to college or university and may make your life easier once you've started.

Organising your time

"Since I've started university I've tried really hard but I just keep getting poor grades. The most annoying thing is that it isn't because I can't do the work – it's because I can't keep track of time! I constantly end up being late for lectures and missing the most important information because I've left the house too late or forget what time I am supposed to be there. I even forget when my assignments are due in and then hand them in late. I don't mean to do these things but I just don't know how to organise myself."

Time Tips

The following are some practical ideas to help you write your schedule or time management plan that incorporates all aspects of your university or college life:

- **Take a piece of paper and write down a detailed term and weekly plan of your time or make a note on your computer.**

Consider five time areas:
- **Work time**: Write down all of your fixed commitments such as: lectures, tutorials, group meetings, assignment deadlines and examinations.
- **Maintenance time**: Make sure you allow time for looking after yourself (and your family). Allow time for meals, domestic chores, shopping, travel, and time to relax. Check that you have a balance between work and your other needs, including sleep, exercising and socialising.
- **Family/friend time:** Identify times for family/friend commitments if this is important to you. Identify when work will be the priority for you and let others (partner and/or friends) know that you are not available at these times.
- **Free time:** You may choose to allocate particular time-slots to particular activities, or vary this according to demands. Mark which ones are important or necessary for you: sport or specific family events, or social activities.
- **Other:** Allow some unscheduled time for emergencies that may occur as deadlines come close. Be realistic with time and add a bit more to always give you an extra bit of leeway.

- **Work out what your targets (aims and objectives) are.** Identify what you need to do in order of importance for the next day, week and month and this term. If this is hard for you, see if a parent, guardian or friend can sit with you to talk through this with you the first time.
- **Put them into your timetable, diary or mobile phone.** Try to have only one system for recording appointments and events which is synchronised to your phone and computer and so is with you at all times.
- **Try to allocate appropriate time for all targets.** Estimate the length of time for each task. (If you are not sure, then ask).
- **Make sure you stick to your plans and don't just end up writing them.** Don't end up using timetable making as a way of wasting lots of time, drawing up 'state of the art' plans and timetables . . . and then not using them.
- **Use your time wisely by:**
  - Using the time of day when you concentrate best for the most demanding work.
  - Utilise small blocks of time for 'busy' but not deeply intellectual tasks such as photocopying or sorting out notes.
  - Reassess your schedule from time to time. Check that you are keeping up to date in all areas. Ask yourself if you need to allocate more time to work generally, or for certain areas, or if you would be

more effective working at different times of day/evening.

- Use 'spare' bits of time wisely. For example, a ten-minute bus journey could allow you to read an article or one chapter of a book for college or university. You could listen on your phone/ Kindle/iPAD/notepad to a recording or watch a video.

- **Use strategies** to remind yourself of strategic meetings or events, such as entering all meetings, events, and lectures into your mobile phone. Synchronise this with your computer so they are all in one place e.g. Microsoft Outlook or Google Mail.

- **Set an alarm** (or two if you are a heavy sleeper!) to help you get up at the same time every day as it helps you become more organised. Big swings in sleep pattern aren't always helpful as well as they can make you feel groggy. Use your mobile phone, alarm clock or laptop.

  - Some apps for this:
  - *http://www.androidcentral.com/best-alarm-clock-apps-android*
  - *http://techpp.com/2013/03/28/alarm-clock-apps-ios-android/*

- **Plan ahead**, prepare for tomorrow, and start this the night before – there always seems to be more time in the evening than in the morning when you are trying to tear out of the door!

- **Make a *short* 'to-do' list every day**
  - Take five minutes at the start or end of each day make a plan of the jobs/tasks to be completed. Restrict the number of items so it remains realistic (five or six).
- **Make a checklist for the week** – organise your day and week so you know what work you have to complete; have your checklist and tick it off as you go. You could keep the list on the wall, or have a book to record things to be done and the dates by which they need to be completed. This could be placed on a corkboard/noticeboard.

  To create your own free online checklist, go to www.checklist.com or use an app on your phone e.g.

  - **Sorted – The Daily Organiser**
    https://itunes.apple.com/gb/app/sorted-the-daily-organiser/id513269408?mt=8&ign-mpt=uo%3D2
  - **24me** *https://itunes.apple.com/PK/app/id557745942?mt=8&ign-mpt=uo%3D4*

- **Build in extra time** – how good are you at estimating how long a task will take you? We often think things will take us less time than they actually do.

  - Always try to arrive at lectures or appointments ten minutes early. Set an alarm to prompt you to leave.

- **Keep regular plans** – make plans daily, weekly and monthly; don't wait until it all tumbles down on top of you and the deadline for work is tomorrow!

  - Develop a pattern if you can to make sure that you do certain tasks each week; keeping regular routines makes tasks easier to remember so that they become a habit.
  - See *www.boxofideas.org* for various websites where you can make your own **electronic timetables**.

- **Use 'Post-it' notes** and attach them in prominent places in order to prompt an action or job that needs to be completed that day. There are also 'Post-it' notes or 'Stickies' that you can download and use on your computer or laptop.

  - *www.post-it.com*
  - *www.zhornsoftware.co.uk/stickies/index.html*

- **Use a notepad**, pocket PC or mobile phone to remind you of what you need to do. Even a small notepad in your pocket is useful.

- **Use your mobile phone to record things** that are easily forgotten or that you might forget to do or create reminders on your mobile phone – take pictures with your phone if that helps you.

  - You could use an app such as Evernote to store them all in one place
  - *https://evernote.com/*

Organising your workspace

"I can never find the work I need and I always end up losing things because my room and desk are such a mess. I want to organise my things but I just don't know where to start".

- **Take a whole term perspective**. Use a calendar, which covers a few months ahead when planning for projects and/or deadlines. Think about your deadlines for this term and also what needs to be achieved overall for the year. It is sometimes easier to see this printed out. For free printable calendars and other useful organisation resources go to *www.freeprintable.net*
- **Notice board** – stick crucial assignments, bills to be kept or exams on a pin board. (Make sure you have pins readily available in a 'pot'.) Or put them all in one drawer or box file.
- **Put similar items together** – try to have a box or drawer to put all of your stationery in the one place.
- **Try to file lecture notes** in the correct file as soon as you get home, or put them into separate trays or coloured box files so you can sort them later. Put a reminder once a week to do a ten-minute sort out. Mark the top of each page with a date and quick code for the lecture. Even if they are in mess they will be easier to sort.

- **Use labelled or colour-coded filing trays** for different information

  - Use different colours for storing information e.g. to read, notes to be sorted, and bills to be paid.
  - Set a time to deal with them weekly.

- **Set up different folders** for different modules on your computer desktop rather than having lots of individual documents cluttering up your desktop.

- **Weekly sort out** – set aside time each week, such as on Friday afternoon, for half an hour to have a tidy up of your notes and study materials. Ask for help if you need to. Sometimes other people find it easier to see what you need to do than you. It may look a bit like a 'sea of mess' and you may not know where to begin.

Websites, apps and gadgets to help with co-ordination and organisation

iGoogle

- iGoogle is your own personalised Google page; it allows you to add all of your favourite websites to one page instead of you opening several different web browsers at the same time. You can organise all of the websites you use most often in one place, including both those you need to complete your university work and your own favourite websites such as Facebook or Twitter. You need to set yourself up with a Gmail account for this.

  - *http://www.google.com/ig*

Applications (apps)

There are many applications available on iPhone and Android phones that can really help you with your studying and organisational skills. There are new ones coming out all the time. Often there are free versions you can try before committing to buying them.

Some helpful ones are listed below:

- **Maps and compass** (e.g. Google maps): With Google maps, you can pinpoint your location on a map so you can plan journeys or find a building. And when you arrive, you can drop a pin to mark your location and share it with others via e-mail or MMS.

- **Find your car:** These applications may help you to find out where your car is parked:
  - *https://play.google.com/store/apps/details? id=com.elibera.android.findmycar&hl=en*
  - *http://appadvice.com/appguides/show/ car-finding*

- **'To-do' lists:** These applications encourage you to stay organised:
  - *http://www.rememberthemilk.com/*
  - *https://play.google.com/store/apps/ details?id=com.anydo*

- **Notepads:** The notepad applications allow you to write anything you want e.g. shopping list etc. Set a quick reminder for your note or share it with others by SMS or e-mail:

- *https://play.google.com/store/apps/
  details?id=com.threebanana.notes*

- **Calculator:** Most phones have in-built
  calculators but there are some others you can
  download:

  - *https://play.google.com/store/apps/
    details?id=org.mmin.
    handycalc&hl=en*
  Scientific calculator
  - *https://play.google.com/store/apps/
    details?id=com. scientificCalculator&hl=en*
  Math calculator
  - *https://itunes.apple.com/us/app/mathstudio/
    id439121011*

Useful websites to help with home organisation

Organisation at home/in your hall/house or flat is
very important; the websites below have lots of
useful resources that you can buy to help you
organise your home and help with daily living:

- *http://www.betterware.co.uk/*
  Betterware has home storage ideas and for
  recycling and outdoor garden equipment.
- *http://www.lakeland.co.uk/Homepage.action*
  Lakeland has many easy-to-use storage
  solutions.

Help with daily living/personal care websites

If you have some specific difficulties with dressing, or self or personal care you may find these addresses helpful:

Nottingham Rehab Supplies
NRS provide a huge range of mobility aids, including aids for daily living.
http://www.nrs-uk.co.uk/

Living made easy
Help, advice and information about daily living equipment.
http://www.livingmadeeasy.org.uk/

Greeper
Help with shoelaces. This has a quick release and fastening.
http://www.greeper.com/home.php

Organising your living space

"I find it really hard to organise my work and keep track of everything at home at the same time. I'm always forgetting to pay the bills and can never keep up with doing my chores around the house. I just wish I knew how to balance everything."

- **Be selective** about the clothes you bring to university or college at any one time. If possible keep many of your clothes at home and change them over during the holiday breaks. Keeping any non-essential items at home can also help maintain order in your room. Less clutter is easier to keep tidy.

- **Cut more than one key** – you may lose it just when you don't want to. It's better to have a spare with a friend or hidden somewhere safe.
- **Use a key ring** that can be clipped to your clothing/belt or bag. A key ring with a buzzer that goes off when you whistle or shout will help you find lost keys.
  - *http://www.easylocks.co.uk/ezlok-magnetic-key-box-safe-disguised-safes-p-3400.html?gclid=CP_OnO6GpLYCFYKN3god5HIAcg*
- **Keep two trays for mail and a bin together** and deal with it as it comes in.
  - Place all incoming mail in the first and open it as it comes through, bills in the second and junk in the bin. Junk mail always seems to grow if it is left lying around; if you don't want it, throw it out!
- **Notice board** – stick crucial assignments/ exams on a pin board.
  - Have a pin board (and pins!) on a wall in your room so you pin up important notices and documents for easy access. It is particularly useful, too, for sticking up anything that you need to do quickly such as paying an important bill, or handing in an assignment.

- **Set up Direct Debits** for important bills if you can – electricity, water, TV, mobile phone so you can plan expenditure.
- **Washing** – Have a laundry basket in your room, which is large enough to contain your clothes until washday!
- **Cleaning products** – Make sure you have some cleaning wipes so that you can wipe down the surfaces in your room. A solid toilet cleaner that automatically works when you flush every time may be easier to use.
- **Bin** – Try to put the bin in a place that makes it easy to throw rubbish into it.
- **Weekly schedule** – Try to set aside the same time each week when you do tasks such as washing, shopping, cleaning, sorting your notes etc. Try to stick to this routine for at least one month then make changes if needed.

Organising your work

- **Colour folders for each subject** – Create a folder on your computer for each subject so that you can file any notes or materials easily.
- **Folder for loose notes** – Keep a plastic wallet or folder in your bag at all times so you can put any loose papers into it. This will help prevent papers being lost. Make sure you clear this out during a weekly sort out.
- **Subject details page** – Create a page for each subject with the subject name and code, your tutor's contact details and assignment and

exam dates so that you have them handy if you need them. Stick this page to the front of each box file for easy reference.

- **Create assignment templates** – Find out what an assignment should look like and make a template for the front cover etc. so you don't need to start from scratch every time for each subject area. Ask for some examples if you are uncertain.
- **Allow regular breaks** when trying to complete study tasks. Break them down into smaller parts or 'chunks' rather than trying to do everything all at once. Don't work solidly for more than an hour at a time and give yourself a movement break to make a drink or go for a short walk after each hour.
- **Plan and give yourself a treat** when you reach your targets.
- **Ask a friend or supervisor/mentor/student support services/student counsellor** – If it is all getting too much and you feel overwhelmed, ask for help; don't wait and worry about it – it won't disappear and it could get worse if you don't do anything about it.

Organising you and your 'stuff'

Some people find aspects of personal care challenging such as being able to fold clothes, or iron them.

The following are some practical ideas that may be of help.

Clothes

- Look for non-iron, easy fold fabrics.
- When washing them, hang them up while wet.
- Patterned fabrics mask stains/marks better than plain ones.
- Buy clothes with few or no fastenings, such as trousers/shorts with easy fastenings and t-shirts/polo shirts.
- Storing trousers, shorts and shirts on clothes hangers and hanging them up helps keep clothes crease free.
- Try using separate baskets or drawers for storing underwear and socks.
- Buy all the same colour or two different colours of socks, so if you lose one you should still be able to find a pair.
- Match your clothes to the event/activities – ask if uncertain. If you are uncertain how to match colours etc. avoid wearing more than two colours apart from black, beige and white which can be worn with them.
- If you have difficulty with new fastenings/ buttons, practise them when you are not wearing the clothes.
- If you have poorer co-ordination when dressing/undressing, make sure you are in a balanced position. Dressing while sat on the floor may make the task easier.
- Make sure you use deodorant and change clothes regularly. Smelly is never a great idea!

Teeth

- An electric toothbrush may be easier to be more thorough.
- Have your teeth regularly checked and cleaned by a dentist or hygienist.
- Use an anti-bacterial mouthwash.
- For fresh smelling breath when out keep some sugar-free chewing gum or mints with you.
- Bad breath is never great for making friends!

Shaving/hair removal

- Electric shavers can be easier to use than a hand shaver.
- Choose a shaver that has a built-in safety guard.
- Use shaving foam, because you can see where you have shaved.
- A good magnifying mirror will make it easier to remove facial hair.
- If it is a big problem for you, consider having laser removal, which is permanent.

Bathing/showering/toileting

- Using toilet wipes after using the toilet can be more effective than standard toilet paper. These are available from most supermarkets.
- If your balance is poor consider having a seat fitted in the shower. Having a strong handrail fitted by the bath/shower may also be useful.

- A bath mat placed in the bath/shower will ensure you don't slip.
- A long-handled sponge will help you wash areas of your body which may be harder to reach.
- If turning taps on/off is hard try long-handled tap turners.
- If showering is difficult – use shower crème etc. in the bath and have a soak.
- Put on a towelling robe afterwards if towelling yourself dry is hard to do.
- Tidy the bathroom after you i.e. fold your towel, and put the bath mat over the bath or on the radiator. Leaving soaking towels and a wet floor is not good if you are sharing with others.

Eating and drinking

If co-ordination is harder for you:

- Try not to over fill cups with too much liquid.
- Using cups with larger handles provides a better grip.
- A kettle tipper may help make pouring easier and safer.
- Use non-stick matting or a damp dishcloth under plates to stop them moving.
- Use an electronic can opener.
- Sit down to eat when possible – it's usually less messy.

Staying fit and looking good

- Integrate activities that will improve your general fitness into your lifestyle, e.g. walk to the shop, walk up stairs rather than using the lift in shops, go for a short walk regularly, go swimming once a week/fortnight.
- Try non-competitive sports and evening classes such as swimming, walking, yoga, Tai Kwando and other martial arts.
- Understand that it may take you longer than your peers to learn a new activity or skill.
- Joining an evening or day class to learn or improve a hobby or skill can offer an opportunity for making new friends. It can be an opportunity to meet others with similar interests and allows conversation to be natural and focused on a shared interest.
- If you are nervous of meeting others you could start by using the Internet as a means of gaining confidence and talking to others.
- There are some tools that can assist you to get fit and track your progress:
  - Nike+ SportWatch tracks time, distance, pace, heart rate and even the number of calories you've burned, but you do have to pay for this.
  - *http://www.loseit.com/what-is-lose-it/* is an app which sets a daily calorie budget, tracks your food and exercise, and may help you to stay motivated and achieve your goal.

Make-up

- A make-up lesson is a useful way of finding out what colours and styles suit you. You will also receive tips on easy ways to apply make-up. Go to a large department store – they may offer this free.
- Some make-up can be easier to use than others e.g. tinted moisturisers as an alternative to foundation, lip glosses as an alternative to lipstick and crème eye-shadow which can be applied with fingers instead of powder which usually requires a brush application.
- If you like to use mascara but find it hard to put on, then think about having your eyelashes dyed instead. This only needs to be done a few times a year and will save on time and daily smudging mistakes.
- Make sure you are sat down in a well-balanced position before starting to apply make-up. If your balance is poor, your ability to do any fine/fiddly task will be reduced.
- Putting make-up on in a set order will help it become a routine and habit. This will also help reduce mistakes.
- Using a good magnifying mirror can make it easier to see what you are doing.
- Restrict the number of colours for eye shadow and lipstick. This makes it easier to get it right. Stick to colours that complement your skin tone and eye colour rather than the colour of your clothes.

- Remember, usually too little make-up is better than too much.
- It is also important to remove make-up thoroughly at the end of the day. Using facial wipes rather than cleansers and cotton wool will save time.
- If you still don't feel confident about your hair or make-up then try asking a friend to give you feedback.

Hair

- Having a haircut that is easy to style can save you time and effort.
- There are many different styling products available now that make styling hair easier to do. Look for blow-dry sprays and straightening lotions to save styling time.
- A style that can be almost dried with 'rough drying' first and then finished off with hair straighteners or some styling products to keep it in place is easy to manage.
- Using a long-handled hairbrush and/or comb can help you reach and look after the back of your hair.
- Longer hair can be tied up or held back using a hair clip.

Eyebrows

- If you want to shape your brows then let someone else do this for you if you have poor co-ordination skills, and then you can maintain the shape yourself. A local beautician or hairdressing salon will be able to do this for you. They can be plucked, waxed or threaded.

- A magnifying mirror will make it easier to see what you are doing.

Shaving/hair removal

- Shaving legs may be easier if you sit down on the floor, on the edge of the bed or the toilet seat. If done while standing in the shower you may feel unstable and this could lead to an accident.
- Consider visiting a salon/spa for regular waxing to limit the amount of hair removal you have to do yourself.

Menstruation

- If balance, fine motor control, body awareness, and organisation are problematic then menstruation may be difficult to manage.
- Stick-on pads (without side panels or wings) are easier to place and dispose of than tampons.
- If using tampons for the first time, start to put the tampons in while in a squatting position or on the toilet as this gives more stability than standing up.
- Some people need a reminder to change their pads/tampons. A watch or mobile phone with a timer set to go off every few hours can help.

Sexual health

Contraception

Going away may be an opportunity to meet a partner. If you want to have sex then make sure you are using contraception to protect you from sexually transmitted diseases (STDs) and also against an unwanted pregnancy. There are many different forms of contraception and what works for one person may not work for another so it is important for you to explore the best option for you. You could do this by visiting your local nurse, family planning clinic or GP.

Some forms of contraception may suit you better than others, for health or practical reasons e.g. you may have thought about taking the contraceptive pill, but if you feel that you may keep forgetting it (and it needs to be taken at the same time each day) then it could be worth you looking for a method that doesn't rely on your memory (e.g. the implant/contraceptive injections).

Here are a brief description of the different types of contraception that are available:

Condoms

Condoms are the only form of contraception that actively protect against pregnancy and STDs including HIV. They are available for free in your local family planning clinic or genitourinary medicine (GUM) clinic but you can also buy them from your local pharmacy or supermarket.

Contraceptive injection
The contraceptive injection can protect you against pregnancy for up to 12 weeks, depending on the type of injection you decide to use. It can be very useful for women who may not remember to take the pill every day.

The contraceptive pill
The contraceptive pill needs to be taken on a regular basis so you may need use a reminder system to take it. The combined pill contains both oestrogen and progesterone and needs to be taken within 12 hours of the same time each day. The mini-pill has only progesterone in it and needs to be taken at the same time each day.

The implant
The implant is put under the skin of your upper arm and steadily releases progesterone into your bloodstream. When it is put in you are given a local anaesthetic, and then have the implant placed in; it will then last for around three years. You can have the implant removed at any time. It is particularly useful for people who know they won't want to get pregnant for a while.

The patch
This is a sticky patch that is placed on your upper arm, shoulder or bottom for a whole week. You can wear them for three weeks in a row but after three weeks you should give yourself a patch free week.

You're protected right away if you use it on the first day of your period.

Diaphragms/caps
Diaphragms/caps are a silicone/rubber flexible dome that is inserted into the vagina before sex. It has to be left inside for about six hours after sex to ensure sperm cannot pass through the cervix.

An intrauterine device (IUD/IUCD)
An IUD (previously known as a coil) is a small T-shaped plastic and copper device that's inserted into your womb by a specially trained health professional. It can last up to ten years depending on the type you decide to use.

Tips to help you remember to take your pill:

- Use a watch or mobile phone that allows you to set a timer/alarm.
- A buzzer reminder or a talking alarm clock can also be used as a reminder to take the pill each morning after waking up. If it is part of a sequence of other activities, like teeth cleaning, it is less likely to be forgotten.
- Try to keep a spare packet in your make-up bag/purse etc. in case you end up going somewhere else and forget.
- Place 1–2 pills in a pill holder on your key ring.

To find out more about contraception go to your local family planning clinic or GP. Or alternatively you could visit the sites below:

http://www.nhs.uk/Conditions/contraception-guide/ Pages/contraception.aspx

http://www.fpa.org.uk/

Sexually transmitted diseases (STDs)

Although there are lots of different types of contraception available that protect you from pregnancy, they do not protect you from getting **sexually transmitted diseases** (STDs). STDs are diseases that are mainly passed from one person to another during sex. Condoms are the *only* form of contraception that actively protect against pregnancy and STDs, including HIV, so it is important that you use them in addition to the other contraception that doesn't protect you against STDs.

There are various types of sexually transmitted diseases that have completely different symptoms, e.g. Chlamydia. There may be no obvious symptoms but if left untreated they can cause serious health issues. If you are worried that you have an STD then you should visit your local doctor or genitourinary medicine (GUM) clinic straight away.

For more information on STDs visit:

*http://www.thestudentroom.co.uk/wiki/Sexually_
Transmitted_Diseases_-_information*

*http://www.thestudentroom.co.uk/wiki/What_to_
expect_at_the_GUM_clinic*

http://www.thestudentroom.co.uk/wiki/Smear_Tests

CHAPTER 4

Independent Living

The move to further or higher education may mean a move away from home for the first time. Being able to care for yourself and live alongside other students can be challenging if you are not so aware of the rules.

This chapter provides information and advice for students who are moving away from home for the first time.

> "I have never lived on my own before, so I'm not used to doing my own shopping, cooking, cleaning or paying for bills."

If you have always lived at home and not had to balance looking after yourself and your studies it can feel a challenge having to manage all this for the first time.

Students, especially with Specific Learning Difficulties, often find juggling work and home quite hard to do. It may feel like a juggling act with all the balls up in the air. If one falls down then they all seem to do so.

The trick in coping at college and university is to be aware that every one of these balls i.e. things you need to do at home and college/university work are all important to keep an eye on. If you don't do this, then home life can impact on your work life and vice versa.

Many of the ideas in this chapter may seem trivial but getting the small things right and automating them, i.e. doing them regularly so you don't need to think about them, can make a big difference.

Starting with the home stuff early before going to college or university means that when you get there you are already confident in doing these tasks.

Setting house rules

- Clean up after yourself – there is nothing worse than someone leaving their trail of mess behind them and then seemingly not caring. Some people with Specific Learning Difficulties find it hard to prioritise and see what needs to be done in an efficient way. If this is hard for you ask your flat/house mates if you can sit down and draw up a list of chores, so you have this to follow.
- If you share a bath/shower/toilet – clean it after you have been in it.
- Wash down surfaces in the kitchen if you have cooked and prepared food. Wash up pans as well and don't leave them to the next day or for someone else to find.
- Don't walk through the house/flat in dirty shoes or boots. If everyone agrees, take them off at the front door.
- Have a weekly 'house' meeting to talk through

any issues calmly, rather than wait for it all to erupt.

- Be aware of other people around you and what bothers them e.g. when do they like to be in bed; what time do they get up?
- If you have someone to stay and you are sharing accommodation – don't let them outstay their welcome – make sure they only use your food etc.
- Sort out where you leave house keys – a tray at the door can be useful, but be careful that key rings are easily identifiable – so you don't end up taking someone else's keys.
- Decide between you where a spare key is kept – under the plant pot is not a good idea!
- You may want to consider having a house kitty for essential items such as milk, bread, butter, sugar etc.

Home maintenance
If you are renting a house or flat:

- Make sure you know where the water and gas meters are and how supplies can be turned off.
- Make sure you know where the electricity fuse board/box is in case the electricity goes off.
- Keep a torch with working batteries near the front door.
- Make sure you know basic first aid e.g. how to look after cuts, burns and scalds (it is always useful to have some plasters in a drawer).

Day-to-day Chores

> "My house is a complete mess – I never know where anything is and I'm always losing things."

Everyone in shared accommodation needs to do their 'bit'. You cannot rely on the 'tidy one' in the house to do all the work. It often causes real problems if this is not sorted out.

Taking care of your chores is one of the main responsibilities that come with moving away from home. Each week you will need to complete certain chores to ensure that your house or room remains clean and organised, and you do your part in keeping clean the communal or shared areas of the house or flat.

Using a washing machine

- Learn to use a washing machine before you leave home. Usually low heat (30º C), short wash is OK for most clothes unless they are very dirty.
- Make sure you know what all the symbols on washing labels mean and what washing machine cycle they correspond to.
- Separate out light and dark and wash separately, otherwise your clothes may all end up grey!
- Wash wool jumpers by hand otherwise they may end up shrinking, especially if the temperature is too high or the machine spins too fast.

- Use conditioner as well if you want 'nice' smelling, soft clothes.
- Don't overload the machine with too many clothes. three-quarters full is about right.
- Use washing machine nets to keep small items together.

Ironing/folding clothes

- Choose clothes and bed linen that are made out of easy-care fabrics that need the minimum of ironing.
- Hang up shirts on hangers when they come out of the washing machine to minimise the amount of ironing you will have to do. You can also get non-iron shirts.
- Lay T-shirts out to dry and straighten out creases while they are wet. You will then only need to fold them up and won't need to iron them very often. Get someone to show you how to fold clothes and practise this as well.
- Choose designs with easy fastenings and without pleats and frills.
- If possible buy a cordless iron, as they are easier to use.
- Ironing boards that are wall mounted or rest on a tabletop are more stable than traditional models.

Making and changing beds

- Try turning the duvet cover inside out and putting your hands on each corner. Now place your hands on the far corners of the duvet and then turn the duvet cover right side out. Try practising this at home before you go.

Cleaning the toilets

If you have en-suite facilities or are sharing with others you will need to clean the toilets.

- Have some rubber gloves, toilet cleaner, and toilet wipes. Start by pouring some toilet cleaner around the inside edges of the toilet and flush the toilet. Put some more in and leave. Clean the toilet seat and under it with a wipe and throw the wipe away.

Equipment

- A dustpan with a long handle is easier to use than traditional ones.
- Use a long-handled mop and bucket for mopping floor surfaces.
- A damp duster is more efficient than a dry one.
- Antibacterial wipes are good for cleaning kitchens and bathrooms as they wipe clean and dry at the same time and are then thrown away.

Shopping

> "Going to University is going to be a real challenge for me because I've never even cooked before, someone else has always done it for me. I don't even know what to shop for and even if I did, I wouldn't know how to cook it!"

If you are living away from home, this may be the first time you have had to do your own food shopping. This task may need more organisation than you may think.

Tips to help

- Plan meals for each week.
- Have some basics in the cupboard to start off with e.g. dried pasta, tins of tomatoes, stock cubes.
- Take photos with your phone of any recipe ingredients so you know what you need.
- Make a shopping list of regular items and then have a column where you add the extras each week – have this on your phone so it is with you.

If you have an iPhone/Android you could use a barcode reader application to help you.

This application allows you to add items to your basket when you're on the go, checking out securely on the app or later online.

The updated order synchronises even from phone to PC and vice versa, so it's great for adding last minute essentials.

Tesco, Sainsburys, Waitrose all do online shopping and you can list 'Your Favourites'.

- Buy items as you need them. Don't splash out on stuff you may never use. Many ingredients can be substituted. For example, if you wanted to make a dish hotter, paprika, chilli powder or chilli sauce would all do.
- Split packs of food and freeze portions – this can save you a lot of money.
- Can you have a communal meal with others once or twice a week and share the costs?
- If there is a group of you, you may want to organise web-based ordering. Many supermarkets do this and it may be easier than going by bus or on foot to get your shopping. It also minimises the risk of impulse buying.
- Shop twice a week – if you plan too far ahead, food may go off and be wasted.
- If you're not sure where to shop to save the most money try visiting mySupermarket website (*http://www.mysupermarket.co.uk/*)

    This is a completely FREE website that allows you to compare supermarket prices as you shop and get the best possible deal for your groceries.
- See following page for photocopiable shopping list.

Fruit & vegetables	Dairy & bakery	Meat	Food cupboard	Frozen food	Drinks	Personal and household
• Cucumber	• Butter	• Fish	• Tins (fish, beans, tomatoes, vegetables etc.)	• Chips	• Fruit juice	• Shampoo
– Lettuce	• Cheese	• Chicken		• Peas	• Squash	• Toothpaste
• Tomato	• Eggs	• Beef		• Pizza	• Alcohol	• Deodorant
• Potatoes	• Milk	• Ham		• Meat: sausages, burgers	• Pop	• Shower gel
--------	• Yogurt	• Bacon	• Stock cubes	• Veg	• Tea/coffee	• Hand wash
• Apples	--------	• Sandwich fillers	• Pasta			--------
• Bananas	• Bread		• Pasta sauce			• Washing powder/ tablets
• Oranges	• Cakes		• Noodles			• Household cleaners
• Pears	• Pastries		• Soup			• Washing up liquid
			• Herbs, spices, salt, oil, vinegar			• Toilet roll
			• Sauces (e.g. ketchup, mayonnaise)			• Kitchen roll
			• Cereals			• Clingfilm/ foil
			• Snacks (e.g. crisps, biscuits, sweets			• Bin liners

Cooking

If you are living away from home for the first time you may need to consider how to prepare meals with others.

These tips may be helpful in informing you about effective meal preparation, food shopping and sharing of kitchen facilities.

Recipes

- Learn a few quick dishes that can be made in one pot or in a dish in the microwave. If you make a bigger portion you can freeze some of it to eat another time.

Websites with good recipe ideas for students are:

http://www.studentcook.co.uk/

http://visualrecipes.com/

Try visiting *http://www.bbcgoodfood.com/* where you can type in the food that you have in your fridge and see what you can make with it.

There are also several good cookbooks around for students, such as:

Cheap as chips, better than toast: Easy recipes for students by Miranda Shearer.

The essential student cookbook: by Cas Clarke.

Useful equipment to assist with food preparation

- Food preparation
  - Boards with a slip-resistant base
  - Different colour boards for different food items e.g. meat, vegetables
- Weighing and measuring
  - Scales with large display, tactile markings, and speech output
  - *http://www.asksara.org.uk/group_ products.php?groupid=2304&pkey=633*
- Peeling, mashing and grating
  - Table top peelers that are stable when grating or peeling
  - Handheld utensils with a rubber grip to aid peeling/grating etc.
  - Electric can opener
- Cooking
  - Timers
  - Microwaves with large display or speech output
- Eating and drinking
  - Items with a rubber grip
  - Battery-operated dispensers e.g. pepper mill

For lots more ideas and details of where to buy some of these items visit:

http://www.livingmadeeasy.org.uk/

Planning your meals

Before making a meal there will be lots of things that you will need to consider.

- What are you going to make?
- What ingredients are you going to need in order to make this dish? Have you spices etc. if you need them?
- What cooking utensils are you going to need in order to prepare/cook the food? Have you got out all the pots and pans you need? Put the oven on, if you are using it, to heat up.
- Approximately how long is it going to take to make the meal? When do you want it ready by? Have you the time for this now? Could you make a double portion and freeze one for later?

Washing up and sharing items

Living communally with others means clearing away after you have been cooking and not taking food from others e.g. milk, cereal. This will cause big arguments unless it is sorted. If you are not sure about the rules, ask to meet everyone so you can clarify this.

Try:

- Having easy to use wipes that you can use and throw away to wipe surfaces.
- Washing up items as you cook.
- Keeping your food to the shelf in the fridge that has been allocated to you and label it if necessary.

- Not to take other people's food at all, but if you do 'borrow' some food make sure you replace it and tell them.

Planning for the day ahead

"Every day you can guarantee that I will forget something – sometimes I'm lucky and it's just a pen or paper so I can borrow it from someone else but on many occasions it's something much more important like my bus pass or my phone!"

When you spend the day at university/college there may be many things that you need:

- Personal items
- Travel items
- Food/drink
- Stationary/work stuff

Put a list into your phone, so you can check you have everything you need before you leave the house, and set an alarm to go off 20 minutes before you are due to leave.

Travel – home and away

"I am always missing buses and arriving late at places, I just never know what time to leave or how long it's going to take me to get there."

If you are living away from home you may want or need to travel to see your family or friends.

Try to make sure that you plan this well in advance; ask yourself:

- Where are you going?
- How will you travel?
- What time does transport go?
- Do you need to book a ticket in advance (often much cheaper)?
- When is it cheaper to travel?
- How will you get to the bus stop/train station?

If you need to find out bus or train times the websites below are useful and they also have apps you can have on your phone:

Trains: *http://www.nationalrail.co.uk/*

Buses: *http://www.nationalexpress.com/home.aspx and http://uk.megabus.com/*

Just enter details where you are going and where you are starting from and you should be able to see a list of all the possible trains and buses that are available to you.

If you need to see how far away you are from the bus or train stations or where you will need to walk when you get off then use the website below:

Maps: *https://maps.google.co.uk/*

Another useful website where you can plan your whole journey in one easy step: *http://www. transportdirect.info/Web2/Home.aspx?&repeatingloop =Y*

Driving with additional learning needs

Learning to drive a car or motorcycle can prove to be difficult for individuals with Specific Learning Difficulties, in particular for those with ADHD and Developmental Co-ordination Disorder (Dyspraxia).

You may find it takes you longer to learn to drive than your peers as you have to learn a number of skills and co-ordinate them at the same time.

Concentrating, judging distance, steering and using both hands and feet at the same time while changing gears can be extremely challenging!

In addition, having to remember the sequence of the steps necessary to successfully carry out required manoeuvres adds to the difficulty.

- Start by driving off-road, where you can practise all the manoeuvres without having any other cars around.
- Some people find it is easier to start learning in an automatic car rather than using a geared car.
- Use your mirrors to help you.
- Turn off the radio – the fewer distractions the better.
- Avoid a using SatNav – as you may want to look at the screen more than the road!

- Avoid having a car full of other people if you are not familiar with the journey.
- Check out where you need to go *before* you start out.

Choosing a driving instructor

Seek out an instructor who has taught individuals with disabilities, as they may have more patience and have techniques that would help you.

The British School of Motoring (BSM) offers special courses that cater for the needs of people with Specific Learning Difficulties.

Some assessment centres will assess driving skills in a safe environment in order to establish the learner driver's abilities.

- Ask your instructor to give you visual clues in addition to verbal instructions. For instance, instead of just saying "turn right" they could say "turn right by the church/pub/shop".
- Practise the skills of parking etc. off-road first.
- Become confident on specific routes so you know what to expect before varying routes.
- Consider taking some simulated lessons before starting out on the road.
- AA has interactive activities on their website: *http://www.theaa.com/aattitude/passing-your-tests/interactive-learning-zone/index.jsp*

Applying for your test

When applying for your driving test ask for extra time to complete the theory/written section if you think you need it. Information about concessions on the theory test is available from:

Drive Safe, Driving Standards Agency Special Needs Team:

https://www.gov.uk/government/organisations/ driving-standards-agency

There are books, videos and CD ROMs available that you may find useful preparing for your theory/written test. These are also available from the Driving Standards Agency.

Other Driving Tips

- Mark the right side of the steering wheel with a red sticker and the left with blue for a quick reminder of right and left.
- Use your mirrors to help you with parking – and look for other 'markers' to remind you which way to steer.
- Plan your journey in advance. Consider using reverse maps so you don't need to turn the map upside down on the way home! Try websites such as *http://www.mapquest.co.uk/* or *http://www.theaa.com/* . These can print out instructions rather than following a map.
- Put a clip on the dashboard so you can easily get to the map, but pull on to the side of the road if you are lost.

- If you are lost e.g. finding a destination or service station – stop and ask for directions.
- Parking sensors make a sound when you are close to an object, and so can help you when parking your car.
- Take frequent breaks from driving if you have difficulty concentrating.
- Turn off your mobile phone when driving.
- Cut down on noise that can act as a distraction. Avoid having other passengers apart from the instructor, have no radio on and no mobile phones.
- Using a SatNav (satellite navigation system) may be distracting rather than a help, if you look at the screen and not the road. Don't 'fiddle' with it when you are driving.

The theory test

New drivers have to do a hazard perception test – this is sometimes harder for adults with DCD and overlapping disorders because of visual perceptual difficulties i.e. being able to quickly focus and spot errors visually for example. There are a number of software and web-based programs that you can use to practise this skill before taking the test.

If you have Dyslexia or other reading difficulties you can ask for an English or Welsh voiceover. You can also request to have up to double time for the multiple-choice part of the theory test. If you require more than the standard time of 40 minutes for the multiple-choice part you will need to send in evidence of your reading difficulty to the theory test booking customer services.

https://www.gov.uk/driving-theory-test/if-you-have-special-needs

Budgeting and finance

> "I am hopeless at managing my money and I have so many different bills to pay – I never budget and I don't know what money is going in or out of my account. A lot of the time I even end up going into my overdraft!"

The move from secondary school to higher/further education may mean a move away from home or may be the first time you potentially have a pay packet or a student allowance.

The following information may prove useful if you are renting your own property or living with others.

Calculate how much your rent and bills are likely to cost your whole house each month. (Your landlord or rental agency should be able to give you a good estimate of these bills.)

For example you may have to pay:

- Rent
- Gas
- Electricity
- Water
- Council tax
- Internet connection
- TV licence

Once you then know the total amount, you will need to divide this by the number of flatmates so you know how much your bills come to each month.

Now calculate how much your bills will come to each term. There are approximately three months per term. (So if, for example, you are spending a total of £300 per month, you will need to multiply this by 3 to give you a total of £900 for bills each term.)

Try working this out for yourself by entering your personal costs in the spaces below:

Total amount being spent on rent and bills each month = _____

Total each month multiplied by 3 = _____

If you have a student loan lump sum, put aside this money into a separate 'bills' account each time you receive your student loan and only use it to pay your bills!

Spending money

If you have a separate account for your rent and bills, as suggested above, you should easily be able to find out how much money you have left to spend on food and entertainment.

As each university/college term lasts approximately three months then this means that there are 12 weeks in each term. You therefore need to divide your total spending money by the number of weeks in a term. For example if you have £720 for the term and there are 12 weeks in the term then you need to divide £720 by 12; this will then give you about £60 per week to spend.

Managing bills in a shared house

- Talk to your landlord about the possibility of paying 'all-inclusive' rent and bills.
- Talk to your flatmates when you first move in together about how bills are going to be managed.
- Suggest to your flat/housemates putting a set amount of money into a kitty or shared bank account from where all of the joint bills get taken.
- If you have a joint or bills bank account, think about setting up direct debits with gas, electricity, water and internet companies so you don't have to remember when to pay the bill.
- If possible try making the bills in everyone's name so that everyone is responsible.
- If you can, sit down with your parent or guardian and go through a budget for the week.
- Talk through meals, coffee, joining clubs, going out to pubs and bars, going to a gym, buying a magazine or game. Try and think through what you may be spending your money on and set aside the right amount each week so it can last you the week.

Direct debits and standing orders

If you have a joint bank account with your flatmates or a separate bills account, try setting up direct debits for gas, electricity, water, TV licence, internet etc. Particularly with gas and electricity if you pay monthly you will have a clear idea of your bills without having an unexpectedly high bill turn up! This also makes payments the same for summer and winter so you shouldn't have to worry about paying extra in winter. As a student, at the present time you don't need to pay council tax so that's one less bill to pay!

Financial support for students

Disability Student Allowance

You may be eligible for a range of support at college or university.

Contact your university or college's student support service and find out what they have to offer. You may need an up-to-date assessment of your needs undertaken in the past couple of years. They can discuss with you what's on offer and in many cases arrange an assessment with you, although there may be a cost for this assessment.

Disabled Living Allowance

If you need additional personal support then this can be provided through the Disability Living Allowance Fund. This has changed in 2013. Please see latest guidance.

- If you need help filling in any forms in order to apply for disability allowance then go to your GP who can help you to complete them.
- If you are unsure about what you require and what is available, contact Skill – Skill are a national charity promoting opportunities for young people and adults with any kind of impairment in post-16 education, training and employment. *www.skill.org.uk*
- The "Directgov" (*www.direct.gov.uk*) website also offers lots of advice on disability allowance for individuals; see *www.boxofideas.org* for links to the specific web pages.

Help and advice with managing money at university/college

If you would like to gain more information on how you can manage your money more effectively at university then visit the websites below:

- Universities net: *http://www.universitiesnet.com/student-finance.htm*
- Students at Uni: *http://www.studentsatuni.co.uk/learn_to_budget.shtml*

Many of the banks have specific advice for students and resources. Here are some examples.

NatWest
NatWest provides lots of helpful resources to help students to manage their money whilst at university/college. Click on the links below to access useful information for the specific areas you may need help with:

- General Advice: *http://www.natwest.com/personal/students/g5/ student-essentials.ashx*
- Help with budgeting: *http://moneysense.natwest.com/schools/ students/planning-your-future*

Online banking – Lloyds TSB
Whilst at university/college, you may decide that it is easier to sort out your bills online. Lloyds TSBClick have made an online demonstration on how to bank online, including paying bills and transferring money. If you think you may like to look at this to gain a general idea of how online banking works then visit the link below:

http://www.lloydstsb.com/new_internet_banking_ demo/index.html?WT.ac=IBIBD0810

iPhone app – Spending tracker – user friendly Personal Finance app.

CHAPTER 5

Study Skills

Throughout your university or college course you will probably have to complete many assignments and exams so having good study skills is very important.

This chapter provides you with lots of help and advice on note-taking, revising, assignment writing and making presentations.

It helps you to learn how you can make the most of your lectures or seminars.

"I find it so hard to take notes in lectures, there is just too much information to take in and I never know how to organise it all."

"I always take lots of notes in my lectures but when I get home I just leave them in my bag and when I look over them weeks later none of it makes any sense to me."

Getting the most from lectures, tutorials and seminars

For many students, university or college may be their first experience of having to take notes in a lecture. This can be a daunting experience. Usually writing down every word the lecturer says is not very efficient but it's difficult to know the best way to note-take.

- In many universities/colleges, notes/PowerPoint slides will be posted on the department's intranet system. Try downloading these **before** the lecture as a handout. This means that you have a chance to read through and become familiar with the topic before the lecture. You can then annotate (add to) the handout rather than starting from scratch.
- To get the most out of lectures, a balance between listening carefully (active listening) and taking notes is needed.
- Some students with Specific Learning Difficulties find doing both of these at the same time quite hard to do e.g.
  - writing notes
  - paying attention for a length of time
  - spelling the key words
  - understanding the information when given orally and at speed.

Active listening

Active listening involves asking questions before, during and after lectures, talks, tutorials, seminars and/or lessons. This will help you get the most out of your studies and help you to concentrate. However you need to do this appropriately as:

- endless interruptions will irritate other students and the lecturer
- dominating the lecture or tutorial will also be annoying.

Before the seminar or lecture take 2–3 minutes to think about:

- What do I want to get out of the talk/lecture/tutorial?
- How does this lecture or seminar fit into the rest of my course?
- What do I already know about the topic?
- Will the lecture or tutorial assist with understanding, help with assignment writing or an examination?
- Are you uncertain of previous work and need clarification – a large group setting is usually not the place to do this. Ask your tutor or lecturer when is an appropriate time to meet or email and make a request.

During the lecture, lesson or tutorial:

- Do you know the main topic(s) being covered?
- What are the key points – often these are told to you in the first few minutes – the lecturer may say these are 'the aims'?
- Can you relate this information to something you already understand about the topic?
- What do you need to know for a prospective assignment/exam?

Staying focused

1. **Reduce distractions** – Sit where you won't be easily distracted, i.e. not in the sun or near a window. Sit where you can see the tutor and visual aids clearly. Make sure you've been to the toilet before the start of the lecture and take water in to drink during the session.

2. **Overview** – During the talk/lecture, take note of the initial overview given at the start and any **key words** which summarise the main aims of the lecture.

3. **Key words** – Listen for phrases such as:

   - "It's vital that ..."
   - "The key is ..."
   - "There are three main ..."
   - "Today we are covering the following areas ..."
   - "You will be expected to know ..."

4. **Body language** – Show YOU are alert and interested. Positive body language such as your facial expressions, movements and posture, help you keep focused and help your brain absorb and retain information. Chew gum if this helps you to focus! If you look alert you are more likely to stay alert.

Tips for note-taking

- **Notebook** – If you have trouble finding your notes, try getting different coloured notebooks where you can write each subject in the order they happen. Some notebooks already have dividers so you can have one section for each subject.
- **Template for notes** – Try setting up a template on your computer with the subject title, date and title of the lecture. Print off this page prior to going to your lecture so that you have a framework for taking your notes.
- **Use a recording format that suits your style of learning** such as: bullet points, visual imagery, flow charts or spider diagrams etc. Keep them clear, simple and short as this will also make revision easier. You may want to invest in a digital recorder device that will allow you to record some lectures. This means that you can listen to them again at a later date and can go back and check anything you may have missed.
- **Use a note pad or computer** – Try using 'autocorrect' for key words that you find hard to spell (this is built into Microsoft Office).
- **Highlighting** – It may be a good idea to take a few different coloured pens or highlighters to lectures to help you note-take. Using coloured pens or highlighters can be useful as they allow you to highlight key words and the main points of a lecture. This then makes it easier to extract

these points when you are writing an assignment or revising for exams.

- **Use abbreviations** – Abbreviations save time. Use them in your notes, but not in assignments. Maybe introduce a few at a time, so that your notes make sense and keep a 'key' to your abbreviations near you until you know them.
- **Leave space** – Leave space in your notes, and a wide margin, so that you can add new information and ideas later. (This is much quicker than rewriting your notes to incorporate new information.)
- **Label and number pages** and write course name and date as well.
- **Glossary of terms** – Look for any words you are unfamiliar with and create a glossary of these terms with brief definitions. Summarise what you have read into a few key points in a PowerPoint slide so that you know where to find the information should you need to reference it in an assignment.

Also try to remember to include:

- Course title or module title
- Talk, lecture or lesson title
- Date
- Your own overview or summary
- Your own additional comments and thoughts
- Any questions to be asked.

Note-taking support

If you are not sure of the best note-taking method for you try contacting the student support service in your university or college as they might be able to offer you additional guidance and training.

You may need to apply for support which is sometimes associated with having a **Disability Student Allowance (DSA)** if you are in university. Your college or university can advise you how to access support.

Let the college or university know if you require additional support as early as possible.

If you are eligible for support you may be entitled to several things to help you with your note-taking, for example:

- A scribe
- Computer
- Note-taking software
- Digital voice recorder
- Audio notetaker
- Recordings of lectures
- Assistance of a support worker.

Scribes

If your handwriting is very poor you may be given a scribe (a person to write for you) for lectures. Giving the scribe information how best to take your notes will make them more useful to you.

Things to consider when working with a scribe are:

- What format do you like the notes to be taken in e.g. bullet points, large spaces between text for you to add your own notes afterwards, typed?
- The paper size and colour you prefer. Do you want lined/unlined/a certain colour of paper?
- How you will store your notes. Think about setting up a filing system from the start.
- If the scribe has an electronic note-taker they could transfer the notes they have written straight on to your computer. They will need to write on special paper using an electronic pen to capture, store and share handwritten drawings, sketches, notes and memos.
- Do you want to record your lectures? Doing this will allow you to re-listen to the lecture whilst reading your scribe's notes at the same time. Some mobile phones may already have a voice recorder that you could use or you could get yourself a Dictaphone. Digital Dictaphones allow you to organise your recordings into different folders which can then be transferred to your computer.
- Give your scribe feedback – they will only know what you prefer if you tell them!

Computer/laptop/notebook

- If your handwriting or spelling is poor you may want to consider using a laptop or notepad in lectures. This allows you to automatically bullet key points and will mean that it's easier to re-arrange your notes after a lecture as you can easily copy/delete/add points rather than re-writing notes.
- Using a laptop can allow you also to use 'auto text' on the computer and pre-type in a series of often used words. If you start to spell the first few letters it will then spell the rest for you. This is really useful if you tend to spell the same words wrongly over and over again.

Useful abbreviations guide for note-taking:

Abbreviations are very useful to use in lectures so that you are able to record information more quickly. (See table of abbreviations on the next page.)

→	Leads to Causes Produces
↑	Increase Rise, Up Growth
↓	Decrease Fall, Down Lowering
~	About Approximately
<	Less than Smaller than
>	Greater than Larger than
%	Percent
Ft	Foot, feet
∴	Therefore
∵	Because
w/	With
w/o	Without
Cf.	Compared to By comparison with
K	Thousand
m	Million

Communicating with tutors and lecturers

University and college is very different from school; not just in the way of socialising with friends but also how students communicate with their lecturers and/or tutors.

A student's relationship with their lecturer is very different from a pupil's relationship with their schoolteacher.

Lecturers usually teach a lot more students at any one time and therefore may not be as close to their students as teachers would be, for example, lecturers probably won't be familiar with your name or your particular learning style like teachers would be.

A lecture theatre is also very different from a classroom and lectures are essentially a time for listening to information and learning about new topics, consequently, students do not usually ask for help in lectures and don't ask lots of questions unless they are prompted to do so by the lecturer. Even though you will not get to speak to your lecturer much during the lecture, they are usually still happy to help answer your questions after the lecture or at a time agreed with both of you. If you want to ask some questions and you are not so sure then send an email and ask when you can talk.

Despite everyone usually being an 'adult' in college or university behaving both appropriately and respectfully is still important. Avoid asking personal questions about someone's family/ personal life unless the person volunteers this information. Think about when you send emails and the number of emails you are sending to ask for help – the lecturer or tutor also has their own life outside of work! Check and ask if you are not sure what is appropriate.

Use the diagram below as a quick guide to communicating in lectures:

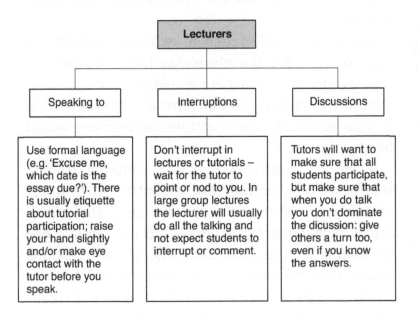

Group working

Some courses require you to work in a group with others to complete certain assignments. This can sometimes be difficult as some people may dominate the assignment and want to do more than others whilst some people may fail to attend group meetings and not meet the expectations of the group.

- In your first meeting try and decide on who will do what, when you'll meet and how you'll communicate. Deciding on these things from the outset means that everyone is clear about what they have to do, therefore the assignment becomes a shared responsibility of the group.
- Arrange the next meeting before you leave.

Assignments

"When writing assignments I never know where to start and my work doesn't seem to have any structure! I have lots of good ideas but I just can't seem to get them down on paper properly."

Try different techniques out and see which style of writing you prefer.

- **Record your ideas**
  - You could record your ideas onto a mobile phone, music player or Dictaphone, so that you can think freely about what you want to write. Then play this back as you are writing your assignment to help you recall your ideas.

- **Talk through your ideas**
  - If you are not sure what to write, then talk to your tutor early on about your ideas to ensure that you are on the right track for your work. Don't leave it till too late (e.g. a few days before an assignment is due). There

may be a deadline when you can submit drafts – check on this.

- **Sticky notes**
  – Write out all your ideas on to 'Post-it' notes and stick them on the wall and then arrange them into the order you want to write. You can use a web based version of these on a laptop if you prefer.

Writing the assignment

Read the assignment instructions thoroughly, try to understand exactly what you need to do – if there are any words that you don't understand look them up so you know what they mean.

- Develop a project plan for each assignment. Use mind maps/flowcharts/ bullet points to help you devise the project plan.
- Create a dictionary on the computer for words that you often confuse or spell incorrectly. They will then be autocorrected when you type them.
- Use a self-evaluation checklist to make sure you have done everything you should, such as referencing, front cover etc.
- iPhone app – Paperhelper. This has your source and paper right next to each other. It splits the iPad screen in half providing you with an Internet browser and a document writer.

Assignment templates

- Create a template for your assignments with a title page, contents page, abstract, introduction, conclusions and reference list. Add page numbers into the footer along with your student number. Have an example of a book and journal article in your reference list so that you can copy the formatting.
- If you want to use a template to help you organise your notes then there are many useful ones available online free of charge e.g. *www.readwritethink.org*
    - **The persuasion map –** This is an interactive graphic organiser that enables you to map out your arguments for a persuasive essay or debate.
    - **The essay map –** You can use this tool to map out your informational essay.
    - **The compare & contrast map –** This is an interactive graphic organiser that enables you to outline ideas for different kinds of comparison.

Useful vocabulary for assignment writing

Introduction
The aim of this assignment is ....
In this assignment I aim to ....

To help you make an argument
I believe that ....
It is clear that ....
It is important that ....
In my opinion ....
It is interesting to point out that ....
Another important point is that ....
On the one hand .... on the other hand ....

Other ways of saying "this means that ...."
Consequently ....
Therefore ....

Other ways of saying "........... and ...."
Additionally ....
Also ....

Other ways of saying "but ...."
However ....
In contrast ....

Words to use if you're not 100% sure about an argument
Some people believe that ....
It could be said that ....
It appears that ....

Referencing guide

> "Referencing is something I never did before university and I don't really understand it. The problem is that I always get the names and dates muddled up and I don't really know the difference between referencing articles, books or websites."

When starting at university or college, it may be the first time you have had to give references about where you have got your information from and report this in your assignment.

Why reference?
You provide references to show others that you have:

- Read and understood other people's work.
- You are not copying directly from others (called 'plagiarising') – be careful of this as you can be thrown off your course for doing this!

Whether you are working on a poster, essay, research report etc. at college or university you have to write down every book, magazine or website you have used (or read a part of).

Tips to help referencing

- Check the referencing style that is required – there are different ones e.g. Harvard, Vancouver, APA – **ASK** which one should be used.

- **Write out examples of the style you need to use** for websites, books and journals/papers and have this at the top of the page and follow it. You can delete your example once you have done your references.
  - **Look carefully** at where full stops, commas, capital letters and italics are. You should always try to copy the styles.
- **Create a reference list as you go** along so you have a record of any texts that you have read.
- **Use a reference manager.**You can put the details into a referencing programme such as 'End Note' (available from *www.adeptscience.co.uk*) or 'RefWorks' (available from *www.refworks.com*), and this creates a bibliography (an alphabetical list of papers, books etc. you have read) for you in any referencing style you require. Many colleges and universities run sessions to help you learn how to use these. It can save hours of time!
- **Use a reference maker**
  - Referencing is hard to do accurately for some students; however, there are tools that can make this process much easier. The link below is a tool that takes in the raw information (author, title, year of publication etc.) and creates the reference in the correct form. You can then highlight and copy this into the reference/bibliography section of your report. (Neil's Toolbox and it is free to

use – *http://www.neilstoolbox.com/ bibliography-creator/reference-journal.htm*)

Proofreading

- Always **proofread** your work before you hand it in. If this is hard to ask someone, offer to work in pairs and read someone elses and they can read yours.
- Consider using a text-to-speech programme. This software lets you hear what you have written; this sometimes makes it easier for you to spot mistakes.
- See text–to-speech programmes and proofing software examples e.g. Claroread and Ginger Software.

Plagiarism

Some people think this is 'just' copying someones work or taking a bit of it and using it in a slightly different way. Universities and colleges take this very seriously and it is important that you can understand what this means and how to avoid it at all costs. If you are 'caught' this can be a reason to ask you to leave the course all together. Most colleges and universities use software that you can put your work through to check you haven't inadvertently quoted someone's work.

- Always when writing about someone else's work don't copy it and if you quote it clearly cite the source and the author accurately.

- Changing the font does not mean it is now your work!
- Changing odd words in a piece to make it 'different' does not mean it is your work.
- Wrongly citing someone's work with another reference won't work either.

See: *http://www.plagiarism.org/plag_article_types_of_plagiarism.html*

Organising your assignments

To help you organise your assignments it is a good idea to:

- Set priorities and time scales, including weekly plans and deadlines, for projects and assignments.
- Stick coloured labels on folders clearly stating title and date of module.
- Use coloured A4 paper for different module notes. Each project could have its own colour so you can easily see which one is which.

Print off and photocopy the template on the next page to help you organise/plan your assignments:

Assignment Outline

Subject/Module:

_____

Assignment title:

_____

Word count: _____

Due date: _____

How long to complete this assignment:_____

Start date: _____

Tasks needed to complete project:

Steps to be taken (e.g. journals from library; list of references; meetings with other students)	Date	Tick completed
1.		
2.		

3.		
4.		
5.		
6.		
7.		
8.		
9.		
10.		

Organising your research report

If you need to write up research/experiments you will probably have to report what you did, why and how you did it, and what you found. This frame below gives the main headings for a research report.

Aim Reason for research and what you hoped to find out.
Hypothesis Hypothesis is another name for a prediction, so this is what you predicted would happen.

Materials

This is the equipment you used. Use bullet points.

Method

This is a step-by-step guide to what you did. You can use bullet points or make a numbered list if you like. Someone should be able to read this and then carry out your research or experiment in exactly the same way as you did.

Results

Your results may be written in a table or as a graph and you need to describe what they show.

Conclusion
This is where you write whether the results support your hypothesis. You can also include ways to improve your research and any problems you've had. If your results didn't support your hypothesis you may want to suggest reasons why.

How to plan an essay

This frame will help make it clearer how to tackle planning an essay at university or college. You may find it easier to create your plan (in steps 3 and 5) on a separate sheet, possibly using spider diagrams or mind maps. The steps should help you to produce a clear, easy-to-use plan, which will help you to write a good quality essay.

1. Read the title

    a. Make sure you understand what is being asked of you. Does it ask you to discuss/describe/evaluate? What subject area are you looking at?

    b. Underline the key words.

2. Create a plan

   a. Write a list of key words

   b. Put together key definitions and their sources

   c. Put together the key sections with headings:

      i. Introduction – You should always start an essay by introducing the subject and saying what will be written in the essay. Keep it simple and brief. It may be helpful to include some of the definitions you have written above.

     ii. Main body – This will contain the argument of the essay. A separate paragraph should be used for each point made. Each paragraph should make a point, back the point up with evidence, and then evaluate this evidence. Use the plan to organise these points and jot down which evidence you'll use to support them.

    iii. Conclusion – The conclusion should contain a summary of the points that have been made throughout the essay. Try not to bring in any brand new information that could affect the conclusions made. In some cases, mentioning other areas of interest within the subject can be a good way of showing that you have widely researched the area.

   d. Put ideas into each section and write some notes where you will get information from (books, journals, websites, lecture notes or handouts).

3. Research

   a. Research the topic thoroughly. This may involve finding books on the subject and looking for journal articles. You may be able to use information given in lectures to look for specific articles or use databases to find articles relating to key words.

   b. **Make sure you keep a record of the sources that you have used AS YOU GO ALONG so that writing your references is simple.**

Using the software and the Internet to help you with your work

"I have to use the computer to do a lot of my course work and sometimes I really struggle – I know there must be things out there that can help me but I just don't know what they are."

There are many ways that you can use your computer to help you with your studying.

The following are some technology suites that are free to use and may be of assistance to you.

EduApps

http://eduapps.org/?page_id=52 is a collection of free assistive technology software, also on the same site My Study Bar

Portable applications are software programs that run directly from an external drive (e.g. USB stick) without needing to be installed on the host computer. This means that a learner who needs to use text-to-speech software, change screen colours, magnify the screen or use an alternative mouse/keyboard could carry their software around in their pocket for use wherever they happen to be, and are not limited by the restricted access often in place in their institution.

- **EduApps**

EduApps consists of useful software collections that are free for you to download and use. (see page 86)

- AccessApps, provides a range of solutions to support writing, reading and planning, as well as sensory, cognitive and physical difficulties.
- LearnApps, as its name implies, is specifically designed for learners.
- MyStudyBar.
- MyAccess, a portal to all your favourite and accessible applications providing inclusive e-learning options for all.
- Create&Convert, designed to help publish accessible information for all.
- Accessible Formatting WordBar, create accessible Word documents.

– All EduApps collections can run from a USB pendrive plugged into a Windows computer. Therefore, they offer a portable, personal solution.

  ○ *http://eduapps.org/*

My Study Bar

http://eduapps.org/?page_id=7

MyStudyBar is a tool which helps overcome problems that students commonly experience with studying, reading and writing. The tool consists of a set of portable open source and freeware applications, assembled into one convenient package. Easy to install, simple to use.

My Vis Bar

http://eduapps.org/?page_id=29

MyVisBar is a floating toolbar which delivers a range of open source and freeware applications to support learners with visual difficulties.

The floating toolbar is a high contrast (yellow on black) toolbar offering six quality applications; Magnify (DesktopZoom, a desktop magnifier), Speech (Thunder screen reader), Write (Q10, a high contrast text editor), Read (T-Bar for colour masking), Resize (change your desktop resolution) and Focus (Sonar ring to track the mouse cursor).

Study skills

Essay planning tools
There are some applications that can help you with essay planning:

- iPhone application: The Night Before Essay Planner app
  - *https://itunes.apple.com/us/app/essay-planner/id356018239?mt=8*

- A good website with a simple web based essay planner is:
  - *http://www.readwritethink.org/files/resources/interactives/essaymap/*

StudyBlue. Makes digital flashcards to put in your definitions, information to learn and test yourself. There are free apps for iPad, iPhone, iPod, and Android.
  - *http://www.studyblue.com/online-flashcards/*

Study Checker. Records your study and break times. You can track how and what you have been doing over time.
  - *https://play.google.com/store/apps/details?id=com.mjsoft.apps.sc_ad&hl=en*

Essay planning Template (photocopiable)

Title:-_____

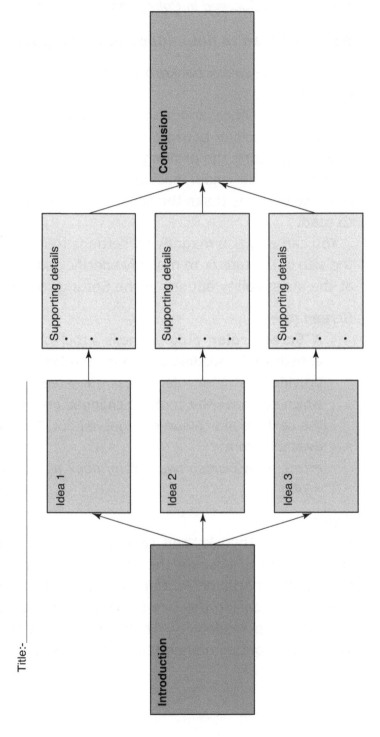

Specific ideas to help adapt your computer

Changing the colour background on your computer

In Microsoft Office and Apple programs you can change the colour background on all documents without affecting the printing.

Changing the colour background to a cream or other colour may make the screen and text clearer to read.

You can also use magnifying settings to increase the size of the font or to magnify specific text – look at the accessibility options in the Settings menu.

Screen ruler

- A '**Screen ruler**' programme is a tool for assisting with reading on the PC and Mac. It provides a strip or ruler across the screen, which can have the contrast changed and have the background coloured or greyed out. This is available from:
  http://www.clarosoftware.com/index.php?cPath =348

Fonts

Some fonts with 'ticks' and 'tails' at the end of most strokes tend to obscure the shapes of letters, so fonts such as Arial or Verdana are generally easier to read. Increasing the size or spacing of the text can also help readability. There are a number of other fonts, but some need to be purchased.

- Read Regular *www.readregular.com*
- sylexiad
  (*http://www.robsfonts.com/sylexiadserif.html*)
- Lexia font which also claims to be Dyslexia-friendly (*http://www.k-type.com/fontlexia.html*)

Text-to-Speech Software (TTS)

With text-to-speech software the person can hear what is written as well as read the text. There are a variety of programmes some are free and some you can try out as a trial version before buying it.
   e.g.

- Natural Reader
  – *http://www.naturalreaders.com/*
  – *www.text2speech.org*

- Balabolka
  – *http://www.cross-plus-a.com/balabolka.htm*

- Announcify for Chrome – you can listen to anything on the web
  – *https://chrome.google.com/webstore/detail/announcify/mmiolkcfamcbpoandjpnefiegkcpeoan*

- Select and speak
  – *https://chrome.google.com/webstore/detail/select-and-speak/gfjopfpjmkcfgjpogepmdjmcnihfpokn*

- Readpal *http://www.readpal.com/one/ screenreader.htm*

- Powertalk – speaks Power Point slides: *http://fullmeasure.co.uk/powertalk/*

TTS software is also more and more built in as standard for new computer word packages e.g. Microsoft Office 2010 and Apple both have accessible packages with free TTS – they have a choice of voices and also allow you to speed up or slow down the pace of the words being spoken.

Proofreading software
These are able to pick up spelling and grammar errors, and words that sound similar but may mean something different e.g. pore and pour. It can also improve word choices by making alternative suggestions.

- *www.ghotit.com*
- *www.gingersoftware.com*
- *http://www.grammarly.com/*

Speech-to-Text Software (STT)
These are programs which allow you to speak into the computer and it types out what you say automatically. These do require some training (only about 15 minutes) and practice to use successfully. A quiet room is also an advantage. Even when the content is typed it is very important to proofread your work as the computer

may not have fully understood what you wanted to say.

- Programmes available include '**Dragon Naturally Speaking'** and '**IBM Via Voice**' available from e.g. *www.microlinkpc.com*
- There are free versions of Dragon to try for iPad and iPhone
- Text-to-Speech; voice to text is a Chrome app
  - *https://play.google.com/store/apps/ details?id=appinventor.ai_hobbypointindia. Text2Speech&hl=en*
  - On iPhone 6 and beyond there is Siri built in and in Google there is Voice Search

Touch typing software
Learning to touch type can be an extremely useful skill particularly when completing long assignments. There are a number of web based programmes which teach touch typing skills including:

- *www.bbc.co.uk/typing*
- *www.typingweb.com*
- *www.nimblefingers.com*
- *www.typefastertypingtutor.com/index.html*
- *http://www.learntyping.org/typinggames.htm*

Examples of some commercial packages available:

- Typing Instructor Deluxe
- Ultrakey
- Mavis Beacon Teaches Typing

You can also download some free apps

- Taptyping
  - *http://ipad.appstorm.net/how-to/utilities/how-to-improve-your-typing-skills-with-taptyping/*

- Typing web
  - *http://www.typingweb.com/*

- Typing test
  - *http://www.typingtest.com/*

Predictive text

Predictive text programs anticipate words and offer suggestions as you type. They also learn words you use often. They are standard on most phones (although they can be turned off) and help with spelling as well as speed.

You can also use predictive text software on your desktop or laptop to help get your thoughts down quickly.

Let Me Type: once it gets used to your style this free software offers suggestions as you type

- *www.clasohm.com/lmt/en/*

Typing efficiently

Shortcuts
Another way to add to your keyboard skills is to use some of the keyboard shortcuts or KEYSTROKES. Learn a few and it can really speed up your actions.

- *http://support.microsoft.com/kb/126449*
- *http://www.autohotkey.com/board/topic/1738-comprehensive-list-of-windows-hotkeys/*

Auto Hot Key

If you are technically minded you can set up a chain of operations from one command.

http://www.autohotkey.com

Presentations

Not all courses require students to give presentations, but at some point in your university or college course it is quite likely that you may have to give a presentation.

Many students find this quite hard, especially if they have never had to make one before. This is especially true if communication skills are not a strength or reading notes aloud is harder to do.

Tips to improve your presentation:

- Look at the people you are presenting to if you can, or focus on something they are wearing.
- Don't speak too fast – it is harder for others to listen to you.
- Use a computer program such as 'PowerPoint' or Keynote to lay out what you need to say.
- Don't have too many words on every slide – four or five points per slide are plenty.
- Use easier to read fonts such as Arial, Verdana.
- Better to keep the design simple so everyone is

listening to what you are saying, unless design counts for additional marks. Too dark text on a dark background may be harder for someone to read.

- Introduce what you will speak about i.e. the aims of the talk, speak about it, and then say at the end what you have spoken about. You can have some notes but try not to read every word (practise this).
- Try to make your presentation tell a story – it should flow from one slide to another so the listener can follow the topic easily.
- Know your topic.
- Rehearse. Time how long it takes you.
- Practice in front of someone else if you can – get them to ask you some questions so you can think what your tutors may ask you.

Preparing for exams

"I am never prepared enough for my exams, I just don't think about the things that I am going to need on the day or the room that I am going to be in – I leave everything until the last minute and then I start panicking because I'm not ready."

"I just don't know how to revise properly – I always find myself reading my notes over and over again but none of it ever seems to stay in!"

Best time and place for you to study

Some people learn best in the morning, while for others the evening is their optimum time. Some people need a quiet environment while others need music or background noise.

Follow the steps below to help you find an environment that is best for you:

1. Find a study area

Where possible set aside a specific place for studying.

Find a place or places where you can concentrate and study and try to build a habit of using this space for doing most of your studying.

Suitable places for personal study include:

- The college/university library
- Town library
- Empty classroom
- Bedroom
- Office space at home
- Kitchen
- Lounge

Some people find that studying where they sleep is not such a good idea, because they find it harder to switch off.

2. Set up your study area

Ensure, if you can, that your study area has the following:

- Good lighting
- Good ventilation
- A comfortable chair with good back support, but not too comfortable so you don't fall asleep!
- Your arms should be at waist height to write or type

In addition you may find the following helpful:

- an angle board for writing to help support your wrists and forearms
- If using a computer make sure the screen is at eye height where possible, so you are not straining your neck
- A book rest that puts the book at eye level

Your study area should not have the following, if possible:

- A distracting view of other activities that you want to be involved in
- A TV
- A roommate or friend who wants to talk a lot and will interrupt you when you are trying to concentrate
- A mobile phone ringing all the time, or texts coming in to distract you

3. Equip your study area
In order to get the most from your studies you need to be prepared.

The following is a list of equipment that you may need to collect and take with you to your study area before you start:

(Many students could keep the first five items on a computer or notepad rather than having lots of paper).

- Timetables and planners
- Text/reference books
- Coursework/lecture notes
- Assignment questions or past exam papers
- 'Post-it' notes
- Pens, pencils, ruler, colours, eraser and pencil sharpener
- Highlighter pens
- Corrector fluid
- Calculator
- Dividers, files, hole punch, folders, plastic wallets
- Rough paper, coloured paper, lined paper, graph paper, A4 computer paper, notepad
- A memory stick to save computer work on (always back up your work or back up to the Cloud)
- Watch/clock/mobile phone
- Drink (preferably not alcohol!)

Where is the best place for you to study?
Think about your answers, there are lots of suggestions and strategies that you could use to make studying better for you.

Where is the best place for you to study e.g. in the library, lounge, bedroom?

Suggestions:

> Try studying in different rooms where you are near people and then away from distractions.

> Try facing towards and/or away from the window.

> If the study environment is too noisy try wearing headphones or listening to some music.

When is the best time for you to concentrate e.g. morning, evening, late at night?

Suggestions:

> Try studying in the early morning, afternoon and evening to see which suits you best.

> Don't study for longer than one hour without a 15-minute break.

Try to be consistent in the time you get up each morning, despite the time you go to bed. Big swings in sleep pattern can make you feel groggy.

What position is best e.g. sitting on the floor, sat at a table/desk, lying down?

Suggestions:

> Sit in different styles of chairs to see which suits you best. Make sure you are sat in a good position with your feet on the floor, especially if you are working at a computer.

What lighting do you prefer e.g. lamp, overhead light, bright light, tinted lights?

Suggestions:

> Some people find tinted lights helpful, but other people find bright lighting helps them focus on the work. Try a variety of lighting to see which suits you.

Are you better hearing information e.g. listening to tapes, lectures?

Suggestion:

> Try listening to audiotapes of your own voice as well as others when you are revising. You can also use text-to-speech software if this helps you to learn.

Do you prefer to read information/course material to understand?

Suggestions:

> If you need to read and see the work try using bullet points and mind mapping techniques to help you summarise key points.

Use a highlighter pen to highlight key words/phrases.

Do you learn better from practical application rather than just listening and/or reading?

Suggestion:

> Try writing/drawing notes on scrap paper as you work, as the actual movement of writing will help you regardless of the presentation of your work. Also try to explain the concept to a friend as this will ensure you have fully understood the topic.

Are you better studying alone, with a group or with a friend?

Suggestions:

> If studying alone, make sure you are comfortable and have all the equipment you need.

> If studying in a group, plan how you will work together, when and where you will meet and what topic you will cover and stick to it. The group should be no more than four people. Create some aims of what you want to achieve and also a time frame to do so.

Do you find it difficult starting studying whatever the time of day?

Suggestion:

> Decide on a time you will start and set a timer or alarm to remind you. Also tell a friend or family member of your plan, as they will help you keep to it.

Backing up your work

- If you use a computer then have a system for backing up your work. Regularly synching your phone with your computer is a must for updating and access.
- **Memory stick** – a USB is portable but can also be lost easily! Put it on your key ring.
- **External hard drive** – this could stay at home and you could back up every time you work on the computer.

- As well as the usual communication tools like SMS, phone and email, there are a number of methods to store ALL your files and work with team members and study buddies.
- **Web Storage**: allows you to use Cloud storage and share information with one or more people through your web browser.
- **Google Docs**
  - *https://drive.google.com/?pli=1#my-drive*
- **Dropbox**
  - *https://www.dropbox.com*

Tips to help improve memory
Some of these suggestions may work for you. You may need to try one at a time in order to identify which ones are most useful to you.

- **Use multi-sensory learning techniques.** See it, hear it, and do it.
- **Understand it.** It's much harder to learn if you don't fully understand what you are reading or what is being explained. Ask if you are not sure.
- **Organise information or 'chunk it'**. Put information into sequences or categories. If you can't see how to, ask someone to help. Categorising work can be hard for some people especially if you have DCD/Dyspraxia or ADHD.
- **Create associations**. It's much easier to learn things that are linked together, especially to something you know already. Think of a word that you can use to remind you.

- **Create visual images** if you can with an object or person to assist with recall.
- **Record your own information**. Read out and record on to tape perhaps.
- **Listen to music while you work**. Try soft music with no words in the background. Vary the music. Listening to music may help to trigger your memory, rather like a cue card.
- **Some people find using mind maps or spider diagrams** helpful for displaying key ideas and facts only. Highlight any errors, and add omissions in a new colour. Then test yourself, from memory; see if you can create an image of the information in your mind.
- **Try using flash cards**. Use key words on one side and meanings/explanations on the other. Test yourself on each card and set aside the ones you know well. Repeat this process. The pile of cards you know well should gradually get larger until you feel you know all the information.
- **Draw the information**. Cartoons, thumbnail sketches, maps, graphs, pie or flow charts, tree diagrams can all be useful.
- **Label, number and underline** to highlight important information. Divide your whole topic into easy to follow parts using your own note-taking style.
- **Try writing your notes out** read them and check your knowledge by asking yourself questions about the information or seeing how much you can recall from memory.

- **Try reading in different ways**. Try reading the information out loud or step-by-step so you have time to process what the information means. Try skim reading it – read over the information quickly to get an overview, then go over it again and highlight the important parts with coloured pens.

Additional ways of remembering information

- **The Think and Link System**
  - Create a vivid image in your mind. A mental movie using objects like: an elephant; a jelly; an umbrella; a bus stop; a frog etc.
- **The Room-Information System**
  - You choose a room and get an image of it in your head. Then give this room a 'fact' you want to remember. You then associate the fact with that room. Remember the room and the 'fact' returns.
- **Rhyming Mnemonics**
  - These are rhymes/sentences which are created to contain information that you want to remember e.g. 'Thirty days has September, April, June and November'; 'i' before 'e', except after 'c'.

- **Acronyms**

There are two types of acronyms:

- **Initial Letter Sentences:** e.g. **R**ichard **O**f **Y**ork **G**ave **B**attle **I**n **V**ain = red, orange, yellow, green, blue, indigo, violet is used to help recall the order of and the colours of a rainbow.
- **Initial Letter Words** e.g. **HOMES** = **H**uron, **O**ntario, **M**ichigan, **E**rie, **S**uperior (five Great Lakes of N. America).

Studying with others

Some people prefer to work in pairs or in a small group when revising. This can be very successful, but you need to be disciplined and formally agree your study rules. Some people find it intensely irritating to work with others as they work differently to them.

If working with other students appeals to you, and if your circumstances permit, you may wish to be part of a Study Group. Consider your different styles of learning and make sure that you all learn through agreed means, otherwise some may benefit more than others.

Organising a Study Group

This could be virtual (using a webcam/Skype/ Facetime/Google-share, or email) or a real group depending where you live and the type of course you are studying. Some people find it easier to work in a 'virtual group' through email or Skype.

A successful Study Group does require experimentation, practice, and perseverance and, in some cases, a financial cost. Your own particular situation, including access to technology and the costs involved, will determine the ways you choose to communicate.

- Email/text other students to share useful readings or ideas.
- Make some quick notes (interesting points, helpful readings, difficulties) about your study, photocopy them and email them to members of the group. Members of the group may respond (a phone call, a copy of a useful article, the name of a book). The next week another member should do the same. In this way everyone receives regular contact with minimal effort.
- Telephone contact either individually or through a teleconference call.
- Skype – you can set up group Skype but there is an annual payment for this.

Expectations

- Whether you are meeting together in a face-to-face situation or using technology to communicate, it is important that on each occasion those in the group share an understanding of what is to be achieved and how that is to happen.

- The initial contact should provide the opportunity for individuals to give some background about themselves so that common interests can be established.
- Format of sessions will depend on the purpose of the 'group'. It may meet to discuss the issues just before an assignment is due, or on a weekly basis to share ideas from specific reading materials, or immediately before a planned teleconference with a lecturer.
- Leadership is an important issue, which should be addressed in conjunction with the purpose of the sessions.
- Though groups can be rewarding experiences, they require thought and careful planning. Difficulties sometimes arise when some people in the group do more than others. Try to set an agreement between you on what is expected of each student in the group.

Organising your revision schedule

"One of the worst experiences I have ever had was being late for an exam, I couldn't concentrate properly because I kept feeling so panicked and rushed, it was horrible. I really need to learn to organise myself so that I know exactly when all of my exams are and what I have to revise."

Tips on making a revision timetable:

- List each topic in every subject, that you have to revise and when your exams are.
- Highlight the topics you know the least about.
- Estimate the amount of time you will need for each topic.
- Mark all exams in your diary and the times they start and finish.
- Draw up a week-by-week timetable with detailed revision sessions, topic by topic.
- Build in spare time, 'flexi-time', when you can catch up if you are behind, but if you are on target, it becomes extra free time!
- Make sure you know everything about the exam – when, where, how long, number and type of questions, if there is a marking grid to know how marks will be allocated (and whether they are compulsory or if you have a choice of questions).
- Use iPhone flash cards to assist with college and university subjects.
    - *https://itunes.apple.com/gb/app/revision-app-ultimate-revision/id451009060?mt=8*

Time to study

Think about when you did your best in an exam or assignment in the past – what did you do?

Exam skills can be learnt, but usually need to be practised.

Tips to help you achieve the most out of your study time:

- **Revise with a purpose**. You are looking for the main concepts/principles/theories/facts/processes to do with the topic area. Sometimes this will involve memorisation (e.g. formulae, definitions etc.); at other times it will mean identifying several major points.
- **Build a set of study notes** drawn from lectures or talks and from textbooks. Some people make up a set of flash cards from their notes with a question on one side and the answer on the other.
- One of the best ways to learn from text books and remember is to use the **SQ5R** method:
  - **Survey** – briefly survey the whole topic and look for summaries.
  - **Question** – ask yourself questions based on the headings in the reference book or your notes (e.g. in biology, for 'Involuntary muscles', ask What are the involuntary muscles of the body? What is meant by involuntary?).
  - **Read** – actively with definite questions in mind. Read only to the end of each headed section.
  - **Record** – summarise five main points under each heading. Make key ideas stand out so that they will 'jump out at you' later. For example: draw vertical lines in the margin next to important content, bracket key ideas,

underline or highlight selectively (on your own books and notes only, of course!)
- **Recite** – ask yourself questions and try to answer them without looking at your notes. If you can't, go back and try again.
- **Review** – briefly re-read and review each summary as you complete it. Make time to revise again, testing yourself by writing and reciting.
- **Reflect** – ask yourself, "What does all this mean? How can I apply it?" Try to make a picture in your mind or tell yourself a story to consolidate the material.

- **Charts, graphs and diagrams** can be important tools to help you summarise information.
  - Ask yourself questions based on the labelled parts and the relationship between the parts.
  - Try to reproduce the diagram without looking, keeping your questions in mind, or by referring to a picture of the diagram in your mind.
  - Check for errors, re-draw, and then check again.

Different ways to capture information

Using Excel

Use Excel to create lists with sections, timelines and notes, add colour, use a different workbook for each year *http://www.youtube.com/watch?v=6IAhk5xZf5A*

Diagrams
Use 'Word' Smart-Art to create diagrams with many levels of branches
http://www.youtube.com/watch?v=AiYPVY55uag

Mind/Spider maps

Mind maps are diagrams with a key word, image, theme or task in the centre. Information and ideas can then be added which branch from this central topic, and can be linked or grouped together using colours, text and pictures.

Some students find this approach confusing and they are not sure how to organise their work and prefer a linear approach such as making bullet points perhaps in PowerPoint or making notes using sticky notes and then arranging them into an order once ideas have been put down.

Mind Maps
You can use Mind Mapping software to make detailed plans with many sub-branches.
http://spyrestudios.com/15-great-mindmapping-tools-and-apps/

To actually make your own mind map online the following websites are very useful; many of them are free or allow you to have a free trial before you buy.

Below are a few that are available online:

- *http://www.inspiration.com/
  WebspirationClassroom*
- *http://www.visual-mind.com/index.php*
- *http://www.visual-mind.com/index.php*
- *http://cayra.en.softonic.com/*

Other programs that have been highly rated include:

- Mindmeister app for iPhone and Android
  - *http://www.mindmeister.com/mobile*

- XMind
  - *http://www.xmind.net/*

- Imindmap
  - *http://www.thinkbuzan.com/intl/
    products/imindmap*

Sticky Notes
Examples of these are already built into Apple and Microsoft programs but you can also download them.
- *http://evernote-sticky-
  notes.en.softonic.com*

Revising for exams

Keep a positive attitude
Remind yourself of all the good consequences of success and take time to recall past successes. If you can't see that you have been successful ask someone else to help you to see this. If stress gets the better of you, remember there are ways of dealing with it. University/college counsellors will be able to offer strategies to combat stress.

Keep fit and healthy
For peak performance keep regular sleeping, exercise and good eating patterns. If you have always avoided exercise, think about starting something new, even if it is only walking around the park a couple of times a week.

Draw up a revision timetable early
Allocate your time so that all topics have been covered separately, in short sessions, before exam week and then again just before the exam. Take time off from jobs or other activities, if necessary and if you can.

Attend revision sessions
If any revision sessions are offered by your tutors make sure you attend them! They often give you very helpful advice about the types of questions in an exam. You can also ask about any topics you feel you didn't understand fully.

Revision overview

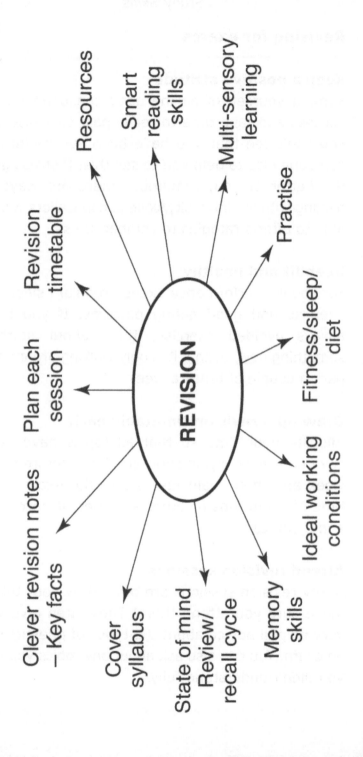

Work with Student Support

Ask Student Support to help you arrange your study timetable. You could also try and work with another student on your course. However do this early so that you have plenty of time to revise areas you are unsure of.

Revision notes

Ask your lecturer for revision notes and any past exam papers. Also look for revision guides or information on your university website. Build enough time into your study plan then allocate some extra time if possible.

Practise past exam papers

If possible ask your lecturer for past exam papers to practise. The questions are often in a similar format so you can get a 'feel' for what they are likely to ask. Try completing these in the same amount of time as you would have for the exam. Use your mobile phone alarm to prompt you to move on to the next section. This can also help you see if there are any areas you need to revise further.

Assignments and revision web programs

For weekly and daily organisation prompts there are programs free and built into your software or in your email system e.g. Outlook or Googlemail.

There is also a great range of free software on a free trial basis to keep you on track.

Download a few and try them out to see what suits you.

http://www.snapfiles.com/freeware/productivity/ fwnotetaking.html

http://eduapps.org/?page_id=52

Some examples of specific programmes include:

EverNote
  http://evernote.com

Sticky Notes
  http://evernote-sticky-notes.en.softonic.com

Clever Notes
  http://clever-note.appspot.com

OneNote
  http://office.microsoft.com/en-001/onenote-help/demo-what-is-onenote-HA010168634.aspx

In the actual exam

"I'm always worrying about exams and just get so stressed about them. No matter how much work I do, I never feel like I'm prepared enough."

"I spend weeks revising and then when I finally get in the exam I panic and my mind just goes blank."

Much exam stress can be alleviated by preparing adequately beforehand.

1. Know the vital information

- You must know:
  - Which exam
  - When it is
  - Where it is
  - How long it lasts
  - The number of questions you must do
  - The marks allocation

- Find out exactly what is required for the test/exam.
- What will be covered and what will be omitted (refer to course outline).
- List the things that you must know and rank them in importance.
- Know what types of questions to expect (essay, short answer, or multiple-choice).
- Find out how many questions, total time, and how marks are distributed over the questions.
- Check whether past exam papers are available in the library or online and practise answering questions.
- Check equipment needed, for example, mathematical equipment, calculator, or texts for open book exams.
- Talk to friends who have done the course before for advice on what to expect.
- If you like you could form a study group and practise firing questions at each other.
- Allot study time in proportion to how much the test/exam counts towards the final grade.

2. Check you have the right equipment

Check you have:
- Enough pens, pencils, colours, rulers, maths equipment.
- Any texts you're allowed, such as a dictionary.
- A watch/clock that works and is accurate.

3. The day before the exam
Don't:

- Revise too late so you can't get to sleep.
- Check where you need to go – room number, building.

Do:

- Check through (skim/scan) notes/typical questions.
- Give yourself enough time to wind down and relax before going to bed.
- Avoid others who are 'panic people'.

4. On the day

- Give yourself enough time to wake up properly.
- Eat sensibly – don't go to an exam without any breakfast; have something filling and slow-burning such as porridge or cereal.
- Arrive in good time; too early and others may panic you but exactly on time can feel too late.
- Have a bottle of water, with a cap to avoid spills, that you can place on your desk.

5. The exam room

- Listen carefully to what the exam invigilator tells you.
- Check that you have all pages, questions, answer sheets and scrap paper.
- Put your watch where you can see it easily.
- Take a few deep breath and read **ALL** the instructions on the paper twice ... even if you think you know them.
- Make sure you check how many questions you need to answer and at least attempt all of them. If in doubt, ask the invigilator or examiner.
- If you have been awarded extra time, check that the invigilator knows.
- Remember to fill in your personal details on the front.
- Once you know which questions you are going to answer use a highlighter to highlight key words in the questions.
- Consider the weighting of marks each question carries, don't spend too much time on areas that carry few marks and then have to rush areas with more marks.
- Allow time for choosing, planning, writing, checking and proofreading. For essays, allow 10–15% of essay time.
- Consider starting with answers you know best. This may help your confidence and leave time for answers you're more worried about.

- Check the time after each part is completed to make sure you are on track.
- If you are short of time, it's better to write an essay in note form than write nothing at all. Write an introduction, outline the argument in bullet points, and then write your conclusion.

6. Multiple choice exams

- If there is a penalty for guessing, leave a blank instead of guessing.
- Read all the options and pick the best and most completely correct, e.g. 'all of the above', rather than one correct alternative.
- Check the terms used to make sure you have understood what is being asked.
- Do not spend too long on any one question – if you are not sure, move on and come back later.

7. What happens if . . .

- Your mind goes blank and you panic:
  - Breathe slowly and think of success. Leave a question if you're not sure of the answer and go on to the next one, or begin with what you know best – anything you've forgotten may come back to you later on.
  - Imagine yourself at home with your books and remember that you DO know the information.
  - Try to think of basic answers to the question like – who? when? why? – until you become more focused.

- Try to answer one question. This will give you confidence to move on to other questions.
- Don't spend too long trying to remember a point – leave a space and come back to it.
- Write any ideas or thoughts on rough paper. Ask yourself questions. Then try the question again. Panic only makes remembering harder.

8. If you are running out of time:

- Don't panic – reduce each answer time.
- Write in note form if necessary.
- Look at the questions that carry the most marks and answer those first.

9. A good answer:

- Comes from a well-revised topic.
- Is the result of a well-understood question.
- Is often anticipated in revision.
- Is planned carefully.
- Is relevant and sticks to the question.
- Is clearly written and makes sense.
- Is presented well.
- Is produced in the way you've been taught.
- Is complete.
- Is checked once completed.
- Pleases you.
- And most of all – answers the question.

10. Is a 'post-mortem' a good idea?

Should you extensively think about the exam immediately afterwards to analyse your success rate?

There are advantages, as you'll gain plenty of reassurance if you think you've done well.

However, there are also disadvantages. If you discover that you haven't done as well as you thought, you may become de-motivated. This could affect your other exams and lead to high anxiety levels.

Concentrate on the future not the past – you can't change it! Remember there is more to life than just examinations.

Study skills websites

- Study Guides and Strategies
  - *http://www.studygs.net/*
    This is a public service that aims to help learners to succeed. It covers all sorts of things designed to help students including writing techniques, advice for exams and time management tips.
- Skills4study
  - *http://www.palgrave.com/skills4study/*
    Find help with study skills, personal development planning, advice on student life and handy tips.
- Waylink English
  - *http://www.waylink-english.co.uk/*

This website is designed to help students with their English language skills. It provides lots of help and advice on study skills, including academic writing and exams.

- Open University
  - *http://www.open.ac.uk/skillsforstudy/*
    This webpage is part of the Open University website and offers advice and resources to help students to develop their study skills.
- Australian educational site
  - *http://www.aussieeducator.org.au/ resources/studyskills.html#inter*
    This website has many useful resources relating to study skills.

iPhone and Android applications for study skills

iPhone Apps:

- **Evernote**
  - This application supports text, photo, and voice notes, and syncs to an online account, as well as Mac and PC versions of the app so you can have access to your notes anywhere. This is useful for backing up your work.
  - *www.evernote.com*

- **Essay Planner**
  - *https://itunes.apple.com/gb/app/essay-planner/id356018239?mt=8* .

- **SimpleMind**
  - This is a very easy-to-use mind mapping tool for the iPhone. The free version lets you create and export Mind Maps in the SimpleMind format, and the pay version lets you export your mind maps in OMPL, Freemind, PDF, and PNG formats.
  - *http://www.simpleapps.eu/simplemind/*

Android Apps:

- **Note Everything**
  - This is a notepad application where you can create different types of notes in one app, including text-, paint-, voice-, checklist- and photo notes. Your notes can be organised in folders.
  - *https://play.google.com/store/apps/ details?id=de.softxperience. android.noteeverything&feature=search_ result#?t=W251bGwsMSwxLDEsImRlLnNvZ nR4cGVyaWVuY2UuYW5kcm9pZC5ub3RlZX Zlcnl0aGluZyJd*

- **Voice Recorder**
  - This application is a handy voice recorder where the data are recorded to a SD card.
  - *https://play.google.com/store/apps/ details?id=com.tokasiki.android. voicerecorder&feature=search_result#?t= W251bGwsMSwxLDEsImNvbS50b2thc2lraS5 hbmRyb2lkLnZvaWNlcmVjb3JkZXIiXQ.*

For organisation

iPhone Apps:

There are many applications available on iPhone that can really help you with your studying and organisational skills. Some of the most helpful ones for students are listed below:

- **Maps and compass:** Say you're in an unfamiliar area and looking for a restaurant. With iPhone, you can pinpoint your location on a map so you can figure out how to get there from where you are. When you arrive, you can drop a pin to mark your location and share it with others via email or MMS. Use Googlemaps to help.

- **iPhone car parking application:** These applications help you to remember where you parked.
  - *http://appadvice.com/appguides/show/ car-finding*

- **iStudiez Pro:** This application keeps track of your entire class schedule and assignments. This includes colour-coding class schedules and the ability to attach assignments to each course that show up on the calendar when they're due.
  - *https://itunes.apple.com/gb/app/istudiez-pro/id310636441?mt=8*

Android Apps:

- **Astrid Tasks/to-do list –** This app encourages you to stay organised.
  - *https://play.google.com/store/apps/ details?id=com.timsu.astrid& hl=en*

- **Any.do to-do list**
  - *https://play.google.com/store/apps/ details?id=com.anydo&hl=en*

- **handyCalc**: A calculator with automatic suggestion and solving which makes it easier to learn and use.
  - *https://play.google.com/store/apps/ details?id=org.mmin.handycalc&hl=en*

- **OI File Manager –** The OpenIntents file manager allows you to browse your SD card, create directories, rename, move, and delete files. It also acts as an extension to other applications to display 'Open' and 'Save' dialogs.
  - *https://play.google.com/store/apps/ details?id=org.openintents. filemanager&hl=en*

- **Remember the Milk –** to-do list manager – you can try before you buy.
  - *http://www.rememberthemilk.com/*

- **Dropbox –** lets you sync and store your files in the Cloud and access them from another Internet-connected device or PC.
  - *https://www.dropbox.com*

- **Evernote –** Evernote is an easy-to-use, free app that helps you remember everything across all of the devices you use. It lets you take notes, capture photos, create to-do lists, record voice reminders – and makes these notes completely searchable, whether you are at home, at work, or out and about.
  - *https://evernote.com/*

- **Diaro –** is a personal diary or journal application. You can note down thoughts, experiences and insights. You can attach any number of images to each entry, making this a good tool to also capture key moments in a day.
  - *http://www.diaroapp.com/*

CHAPTER 6

Socialising and Feeling Good

Starting university and college is a new and exciting experience, but the thought of not knowing anybody can be a daunting prospect.

This chapter is designed to prepare you for the social side of college and university by giving you tips and advice on how you can meet lots of other students and make new friends.

"At home I'm really confident with all my friends because they've known me since I was really young, but the thought of moving to university and having to start all over again really worries me. I don't know where to go to meet other students and what if I don't make any new friends?"

"I've never really had many friends in school and I really struggle to make conversation with new people, I just don't know what to say to them. I really want university to be different."

If you have grown up finding school harder than others then you may find it more difficult to make friends. You may have also been bullied. These experiences may have knocked your confidence.

College and university can be a new chance to leave any negative secondary school experiences in the past and 're-invent' yourself. You can be who you want to be.

The first week

The first week of university/college will be really busy.

- You will be meeting new friends.
- You may be saying goodbye (for the time being to parents and friends).
- Finding your way around a new setting.
- Learning about the course.

First impressions are often very important so if this is the first time that you meet your new housemates then try to be friendly and smile and introduce yourself.

Don't forget that **everyone else is new too**; they may appear confident, but that does not mean they are feeling confident.

Making new friends

Tips
One of the best ways to ensure that you socialise and make friends at university or college is by taking some risks and starting a conversation.

It may seem easier to go home or to stay in your room on your own and hide away, but it is important that you do whatever you can to avoid this situation.

Instead:

- Don't close your door in halls of residence; try and leave it open and encourage people to come in and chat to you as they pass by.
- If your housemates or course mates end up going for a drink after lectures then try to tag along with them and get to know them better.
- Try to invite people out yourself, even if it's little trips such as going in to town, going shopping or simply going for a quick drink.
- If someone asks you to go for a coffee, accept the invitation.
- Join clubs or go to social events where you are doing something e.g. ramblers, debate club, sports club so you have something in common to talk about.
- If you feel comfortable enough you could even try to arrange activities for everyone (e.g. a flat dinner for everyone, a night out bowling/to the cinema or even a course night out to celebrate your first month/term at university).

iPhone apps to do with improving social skills

- There are a list of apps you can try *http://appadvice.com/appguides/show/body-language-apps*

Freshers' Week

The activities available during Freshers' Week will differ from university to university, and college to college.

One of the most common events that universities usually hold is the 'Freshers' Fair'. The Freshers' Fair enables new students to see all the clubs or societies that are available to them. There are usually stalls with shops and businesses offering students store cards and discounts. There may also be banks at the Freshers' Fair, advertising the student accounts they can provide for students (e.g. those with overdraft facilities). Lots of the stalls will be offering free samples so it's definitely worth you having a good look around! However, it is also very important to think carefully about what you sign up to; some things may be non-refundable so you won't be able to get your money back if you change your mind later on.

Another event that your university may provide is the 'Freshers' Ball', which is usually more relaxed than other more formal balls you may have been to and will usually have cheap drinks and have a band playing. You may like to attend this as it will give you the chance to meet lots of other students from both your year and the years above.

As well as the Freshers' Fair and Freshers' Ball, your department may also provide a welcoming event so that you get to meet the staff and other students on your course before the lectures start. Attending this kind of event will mean that you are much more familiar with people on your course and will hopefully make friends that you will be able to share work with in the future.

Students' Union

Again, the role of the students' union can differ between universities and colleges but in general the union offers help, advice and support to students. In addition to this, the union can also offer many advantages to its members such as cheap bars, shops and sporting or social events.

Once you have registered on your course, you should be able to obtain a student union card; most of these are part of the NUS (National Union of Students), which provides students with lots of benefits, such as reduced entry at the cinema and discounts in many of the high street shops.

Clubs and Societies

Most colleges have opportunities to try out new clubs and activities in order to make new friends. You can also visit the place before you start so you are familiar with the layout. Joining new clubs and activities may feel difficult to do, especially if sport at school was hard for you. However, this may be a chance to try something new, meet people and have some fun. Lots of students try out the activities a few times to see if the groups are for them. Be prepared to have a go at something that you may have found hard to do a few years ago.

Some suggestions from students include:

- Archery
- Bowling
- Computer games
- Debating society
- Environmental clubs
- Martial arts
- Music society
- Rambling club
- Salsa dancing
- Sports clubs
- Volunteering
- Yoga
- Get fitter

  This helps both your physical and mental well-being. Many colleges and universities will have a gym you can join. The benefit of using the gym is that an instructor can guide you through the machines/apparatus but ultimately you can work out at your own pace. It may make it easier for you to join in other sports clubs if you can gain some increased fitness and athletic confidence. Just working out regularly for 15–20 minutes a few times a week can have a positive effect on motor skills, confidence and well-being.

Going out ideas

- **Clubs and pubs:**
  Think about what you want to drink before going out and how much. Have some change with you so you can buy someone a drink if they have bought you one. Have some topics you can use if the conversation dries up e.g. holidays, something on TV or a film you have recently seen. If you can't think what to say, you could place some topics on your phone as a stand by (but make an excuse for moving away such as going to the toilet to look at this).
- **Evening classes:**
  Find out from your local college or from the local library what courses are on – sometimes they have one day or short courses that run throughout the year. This site leads to a range of courses full- and part-time around the country: *http://www.hotcourses.com/*
- **Dating agencies:**
  There are numerous online dating agencies and speed dating services – make sure that you check what you are paying for. Always meet someone in a safe place such as a coffee bar or café and let others know where you are and what you are doing. Speed dating can be a good way to practise 'chat up' lines and see what works.
- **Religious groups:**
  If you have a specific religion you may find social opportunities to meet others of a similar faith.

- **Sports clubs:**
  - Tennis clubs and gyms, for example, offer opportunities for meeting others with similar interests. You may want to try out something different such as yoga or karate to meet other people.
  - The more activities you try and take part in, the more people you will meet and the more likely you are to make friends. Remember, everyone is in the same position as you and they will all be feeling the same way as you, so you are not alone. Once you start getting more familiar with people and making new friends you will be out all the time and taking part in all sorts of activities! Just make sure you don't forget about your coursework because you're out socialising too much!

Alcohol and socialising at university and college

Know your limits! Binge and excess drinking on a regular basis can affect your health both in the short and longer term. In particular some people with DCD have described that their co-ordination is made worse by drinking and they appear to be more sensitive to the effects. Other people find that because they may be impulsive they drink before thinking, and then drink to excess, only realising the impact too late. If you have drunk too much, you will be also less aware of others behaviour towards you and may not be able to predict soon enough that you are at risk.

If you are worried that drinking alcohol is interfering with your daily life, then speak to your doctor or use the helpful organisations below for advice:

- *www.drinkaware.co.uk*
- *www.talktofrank.com/drugs.aspx?id=166*
- *www.nhs.uk/livewell/alcohol/Pages/ Alcoholhome.aspx*

Before you go out:

- Have something to eat.
- Make sure your mobile phone is charged.
- Have a number in your mobile phone to call for a taxi if you are 'stranded' somewhere.

When you go out:

- Don't go off alone or only with someone that you have not met before the evening – only go with friends you are sure of i.e. from college/university that you know, including going on a bus or in a taxi.
- Make sure you 'protect' or cover your drink at the bar so it cannot be 'spiked' (something added to it without your consent).
- Try to keep a count of how much you have drunk – and have a limit set at the start of the night.
- Try not to mix different alcoholic drinks.
- To reduce the total amount of alcohol, either dilute the spirits or wine with lots of soft drinks

like lemonade, or drink water or a soft drink
between each alcoholic drink.

- If you are worried about someone's behaviour
  towards you speak to a member of the club or
  bar staff and let them know.

After going out:

- Have some water to drink before going to bed.
- If you feel sick make sure you have something
  by your bed, like a bucket.
- Avoid 'drunk dialling' people when you get
  home.

Useful websites about student life

University and college can be a struggle for many
students. If you do require any more help or advice
then please visit the websites below; they are
designed specifically for students and offer lots of
advice on everything that you will need in regards
to life at university or college.

- The Student Room:
  http://www.thestudentroom.co.uk/
  The website allow university students to share
  academic and social knowledge: from study
  help, to choosing a university, careers.

- Universitiesnet:
  http://www.universitiesnet.com/
  This site provides student advice and guidance
  on a range of issues including: applying to

university, student accommodation, student discounts and student travel.

- Students at uni:
  http://www.studentsatuni.co.uk/
  Everything a student needs to know about higher education: from student budgeting articles, over 5000 student recipes, revision tips and more!

- Need2Know: *www.need2know.co.uk*
  This website gives advice for young people on student life, relationships, travel and more.

- Life tracks:
  http://www.thesite.org/workandstudy/studying/ studentlife
  This website is all about you and your next step in learning, training and work. It has lots of advice on surviving your first term at university.

Anxious, depressed, or feeling lonely

If you are feeling anxious or depressed and this has been going on for more than a week or two you may want to talk to your GP.

- This is especially true if you are:
  - Having difficulty with sleep
  - Crying for no apparent reason
  - Feeling very low
  - Seeing changes in eating pattern – eating more or less

- Avoiding socialising with others compared to previously
- Increasing missed deadlines for work
- Early morning waking worrying excessively.

Your GP may offer you talking therapy such as cognitive behavioural therapy or may offer you medication where appropriate.

For more information: see *http://www.rcpsych. ac.uk/expertadvice/treatments/cbt.asp*

This has some great strategies to assist: *http://www.llttf.com*

There are also lots of organisations available that can help you:

Counselling

This website shows students where to find their nearest student counselling services: *http://www.student.counselling.co.uk/*

Samaritans

Samaritans provides confidential non-judgmental emotional support, 24 hours a day for people who are experiencing feelings of distress or despair by phone, face to face, by email and by letter.

Website: *http://www.samaritans.org/*
Phone: 08457 90 90 90
E-mail: jo@samaritans.org

Depression Alliance

The following organisation works to relieve and prevent depression

Website: *http://www.depressionalliance.org/*

Mind

This is to ensure that anyone with a mental health problem has somewhere to turn for advice and support

http://www.mind.org.uk/

CHAPTER 7

Preparing for the Workplace

This chapter gives some guidance on gaining a job whether this is part of work experience while at college or university, alongside studying or when preparing to leave. Being prepared is essential.

Looking for jobs or work experience

Going to university or college can be a very expensive time; you may have some student loans to cover some of your bills, but you may want to, or need to earn extra money so you can pay some of this back, and also pay for social activities such as going to the cinema or out clubbing with friends. Lots of students need to have a part-time job to manage to pay their debts.

- Look in local papers – there are sometimes set days for advertising specific jobs.
- Ask friends and family – networking is a great way to tell others you are looking.
- Drop your CV into shops and offices – keep it to two pages maximum on one sheet of paper.

- Tell people you meet socially that are looking for a job (i.e. if it is an appropriate moment such as if you are in a shared conversation talking about jobs and work).
- Check whether there are jobs in the university or college helping out at events or open days – even voluntary work can go on your CV and then may lead to a job and shows others you are interested and willing.
- Don't have too fixed a view about what you want to do to begin with. This is especially true when there are shortages of jobs. Getting one job may lead you into other opportunities.
- Getting any job will not just help you to earn extra money but will also help you to develop the transferable skills that you will need for permanent jobs after you graduate. You can tell prospective employers of your experiences.
- Voluntary work is a valuable option to gain experience in an area you are interested in.

Looking for a job, internship, or apprenticeship

The career you choose should be the product of your interests and strengths and the qualification or skills you have, or will gain.

Strengths, skills and interests

Make a list of your strengths and interests and think about what job would suit you. Ask other people what they think would suit you as well, if you are uncertain.

Look out for Careers Fairs in your area; they are a good way of seeing what opportunities are out there and people are on hand to give careers advice.

Work experience and voluntary work

Once you have an idea of what careers interest you, try and get some relevant work experience, shadowing experience or doing some voluntary work.

Work experience and voluntary work are a great way to get a 'hands-on' feel for what a job involves.

Don't be afraid to volunteer for or experience several different roles. All work experience and voluntary work is useful and can have a positive impact on your self-esteem and confidence. It will also demonstrate to potential employers that you have carefully considered your career.

There are different ways of getting work experience or voluntary work:

- Contact an organisation you are interested in, for instance if you are interested in working in the media industry you could contact the BBC Human Resources department directly.
- Contact an organisation that will be able to offer advice on work experience and/or voluntary work and in some cases arrange a placement for you.

- Check out the local voluntary agency in your area. There are a number of websites you can look at e.g. *http://www.do-it.org.uk/* or *http://www.volunteering.org.uk/*

For help with arranging work experience and voluntary work, speak to the careers' department in your college or university and also have a look on the following websites:

- *www.disabilitytoolkits.ac.uk*
- *www.careers-scotland.org.uk*
- *www.gowales.co.uk*
- *www.do-it.org.uk*
- *https://www.gov.uk/volunteering/find-volunteer-placements*
- *www.voluntaryworker.co.uk/*

Internships
Internships/placements offer you the opportunity for a fixed time to gain some training 'on the job'; they can be both paid and voluntary.

They can be useful in helping you decide whether a career/position is right for you whilst you gain useful skills and experience and get to know a sector of work. They may also lead to a permanent placement in the workplace.

For more information and available internships visit:

- *http://graduatetalentpool.direct.gov.uk/cms/ShowPage/Home_page/p!ecaaefg*

- *http://faststream.civilservice.gov.uk/ summer-diversity-internships/*
- *www.milkround.com*

Additional skills and training

Training never stops. When you have found a career which offers you the opportunity to pursue your interests and take advantage of your strengths and skills, it is important to consider what additional training you may require to progress.

Have a look at these sites as they have some good advice and tips on what training or qualifications you may need for different roles:

- *www.careerswales.com*
- *www.disabilitytoolkits.ac.uk*
- *www.careers-scotland.org.uk*
- *www.nextstep.org.uk*
- *www.monster.co.uk*
- *www.jobs.nhs.uk/advice/intro.html*
- *www.learndirect.co.uk*

Apprenticeships

If you are in college you may want to consider an apprenticeship scheme.

See *http://www.apprenticeships.org.uk/* for lots of information about the different opportunities.

Interview tips

Once you have been offered an interview make sure you are prepared for it.

Preparing the night before

One of the hardest things about getting a part- or full-time job may be getting through the interview, especially if you have never had an interview before.

Here are some tips and strategies on how you can perform your best in interview situations:

- If the employer does not know you have some challenges or a disability then they cannot make reasonable adjustments. Think about letting the employer know you have a disability and how it affects you. If you disclose they have to ensure they are making reasonable adjustments for you. If you don't tell them they can't help you. You would be able to apply for (Department of Works and Pension) Access to Work scheme for assistance in an interview if you need someone to come with you or need specific adaptations if this is for a job interview.
- Learn to describe your challenges in a positive way ... "I have xx but I have overcome some of these challenges by yy. I would be good at this job because of zz."
- Make sure you have read the job description and have examples of how you can meet the skills the company requires.
- If you are being asked to do specific tasks requiring writing, reading etc. that may be harder for you to do, you can ask for additional time to do them or a separate room. Find out beforehand so they can be prepared for you as well.

- Know about the organisation you want to work in – do read information on their website for example, so you can show you have done some preparation. Read their mission statement if they have one or something about the company – what they do, sell, etc.
- Prepare some questions you can ask them about what the job entails.
- Read through the directions to get to the place the night before, so you know where you need to go, and make sure you have the correct money for the journey.
- Get out your clothes ready the night before:
  - Wear appropriate clothing for the interview – it is usually better to look more formal than less so e.g. black or grey trousers/skirt and a white or pale coloured, striped or plain shirt or blouse.
  - Wear clean and polished shoes.
  - Avoid exposing too much skin e.g. a bare stomach!
- Make sure you are showered, have clean teeth and smell clean! Wear some deodorant – when we are nervous, we can all sweat more.

First impressions

There is a lot of truth in the old saying: *"You only have one chance to make a good first impression"*.

Studies have shown that within four minutes of you meeting someone they will have formed judgments about you and that these judgments will inform their subsequent impressions, so it is important to make the most of the first crucial minutes:

- It is also worth remembering that even before going into the interview you will probably be under observation by reception staff, so be courteous to everyone you meet. In some businesses they ask other team members for their comments about you and how you behaved.
- Start off with a confident smile and a firm handshake. Practise this with someone else beforehand to make sure your smile is not making you look sinister, and your hand shake is firm but not gripping the other person so tight that they want to cry!
- When introducing yourself be pleasant, polite and businesslike – avoid saying things like "Hiya mate"; better to say "Good morning" or "Good afternoon" etc. depending on the time of day.
- This doesn't mean that if you are very nervous or appear so that you've failed. Try to remain calm. Take slow deep breaths. Remember everyone feels nervous.
- Avoid nervous mannerisms such as fiddling with your sleeve or watch for example – sit on your hands or clasp them together rather than fiddling with them. If you want to hold something have a piece of paper with some brief notes if this helps you.

Body language

What you say is crucial to the success of your interview, but *how* you say it is also important:

- Think about the non-verbal signals (how you are sitting, your actions and not just the words) that you are giving – are you sounding interested and enthusiastic or that you can't really be bothered? Practise answering questions beforehand and ask others for feedback. Listen to what friends and family are telling you – it could help you to get the job.
- Think about your sitting position when you are asked to sit. Usually the best approach is to sit reasonably upright but sitting back into the chair, and it sometimes helps you to feel more relaxed if you sit at a very slight angle to the interviewer rather than face on.
- Crossing your arms and legs can make you appear defensive. Leaning too far forward could be interpreted as an aggressive stance and slouching or leaning too far back in the chair may give the impression to the interviewer that you don't care too much about the interview.
- Avoid any personal idiosyncrasies, such as fiddling with your clothing or jewellery.
- Using your hands when you talk is perfectly acceptable as they can often bring a conversation to life. Avoid pointing or waggling your finger at the interviewer to make your point!

- Eye contact is essential in conveying interest. Lack of direct eye contact is sometimes interpreted as the interviewee being insincere and untrustworthy, even though it may be from shyness. Maintaining eye contact also helps you to gauge the interviewer's reaction to what you have to say, and whether you should expand your answer or be more succinct. If you are not sure how much to look, you could look at the person who is asking a question's ear rather than appearing to stare at them.
- If a panel of interviewers interviews you, then eye contact may become more difficult, but it is usual to look at the person asking each question whilst acknowledging the others with a glance from time to time.
- Show you are listening. It is okay to take a few notes if the questions are lengthy, or if you need to remind yourself of something you want to stress.
- If you are not sure what has been asked, say so and ask for it to be repeated. This is fine to do so. If you really don't understand what has been asked of you, then don't respond with any answer. You could say: "Sorry, I am not quite sure what you are asking me, could you explain this to me perhaps in a slightly different way possibly?"

Their questions

Remember that not all interviewers are experienced

or well trained, and they too can be nervous. However, they will be asking you the questions.

It is your responsibility to ensure that you convey your suitability for the job. With good preparation you will be able to do this:

- You need to demonstrate your knowledge of the job, the organisation and yourself.
- Make sure you have read through the job description – have specific examples prepared of what you have done to show how you could meet the criteria.
- Be prepared to talk about your strengths.
- Consider how you may disclose your difficulties – present them in a positive light in terms of how you have overcome some challenges and the way you have done so.
- You can talk about specific needs for training if there are gaps in your skills – no-one is perfect!

When asking the candidate questions the interviewers are trying to establish the following:

- Does the applicant have the ability to complete the job?
- In what areas is he or she weak? How will the weaknesses affect their performance?
- What are his or her ambitions?
- What kind of a person is this?
- Does she or he have growth potential?
- Should this person get an offer?

When answering questions you will need to address these issues while answering all questions in the most positive way that sells yourself.

The following points may help:

- **Remember that honesty is the best policy**. Admitting, for example, to a period of poor motivation shows more integrity than blaming someone else for a poor grade or poor performance. It is better to present past actions positively as learning experiences rather than cover them up. Although you have an obligation to tell the truth in an interview, you do not have to tell your whole life story. Try to give the relevant parts associated with this post.
- **Be prepared to talk**. Avoid yes/no answers and expand on the answer. Take your cue from the interviewer, and if you are not sure that they have heard enough, ask, "Would you like me to continue?"
- **Try not to talk too quickly.** When nervous we can rush answers and it can sound like you are 'gabbling'.
- **Ask for clarification** if you need it; this will help you to answer the question more effectively and also demonstrates confidence and control.
- **Pause if you need to**. If you need a moment to think before answering a particularly difficult question, it is acceptable to pause or ask for time to think about the question. This is better than saying the first thing that comes into your head.

- **Be enthusiastic**. Interviewers like to see enthusiasm but do not expect a perfect performance. If you make a mistake it is not the end of the world; try to forget it and move on.
- **Don't try to fill silences** left by the interviewers. Silences are rarely as long as they feel at the time, and whether the interviewer is simply gathering their thoughts or, more deliberately, checking your reactions, it is up to you how much and what you say.

Difficult Questions

The interviewer may try to ask you some less obvious questions to find out more about yourself. Some questions, which can be perceived as particularly difficult, include those, which appear to be an invitation to express all your negative qualities, such as:

- What do you think is your biggest weakness?
- What would you say has been your greatest failure?

They may also ask you some questions, which require you to think about yourself in a different way. These might include:

- How would your friends describe you?
- Why is this job important to you?

Listen to the first question here . . . how would **your** friends . . . not how would you . . . be careful to listen to what is ***actually*** being asked.

Sometimes these questions are asked to see how you will react and whether you are listening. The rules for answering these are the same as for any other question: relax, be honest, keep in mind the points that you want to make about yourself, and emphasise the positive while minimising weaker areas. If you don't know an answer then say so, rather than trying to make something up.

The first question: What do you think is your biggest weakness?

Someone might answer the first question by saying that their strengths lie in their ability to think problems through clearly, and that they can sometimes be frustrated with people who don't work logically, though they have learnt to appreciate the different insights that they can bring to a class project. This outlines a weakness but stresses their strengths and their ability to learn from their mistakes.

The second question: What would you say has been your greatest failure?

When talking about a failed examination or an unsuccessful project explain what positive lessons you have learned from it, and try to highlight how these might be relevant to the present application.

The third question: How would your friends describe you?

This focuses on your relationships with other people, particularly those close to you. Your answer could cover your loyalty, your understanding or your readiness to help, e.g. "I think that my friends would say ..." or, "I hope that my friends would say ..."

The fourth question: Why is this job important to you?

Your response should portray some information about your principles, aims and ambitions in life.

Positive endings

This is the chance to ask those questions you prepared before attending the interview. If you are not given the opportunity to ask questions, assert yourself politely by saying you have a number of questions or points to raise, and ask if this is the appropriate time to do so.

Once the interview is at an end, if the employers have not already made the next step clear in terms of when they expect to let you know the outcome, ask them.

It is important to end the interview on a positive note. Thank the interviewers for their time and the opportunity to speak with them. Shake their hands if offered.

After the interview

If you haven't heard from the interviewer within the time frame indicated at the close of the interview, call them.

Ask if they have made their final decision and if not confirm that you're still interested in the job and ask when they plan to make a decision.

If you have not been successful, ask for feedback

so that you can get any pointers on what to improve before another interview. Thank them for their time. You may be offered a position at a later date.

Don't be too despondent, and prepare for your next interview. After all, the more interviews you tackle the more polished you become.

Useful contact organisations

Disability Rights UK

Disability Rights UK aims to put disability equality and human rights into practice across society. They are a national organisation led by people with a wide range of impairments or health conditions and provide a variety of help lines that provide information on a range of issues.

Details: *http://disabilityrightsuk.org*

Disabled Students Helpline
Telephone: 0800 328 5050
Opening hours: Tuesday 11.30–13.30 & Thursday 13.30–15.30
Email: students@disabilityrightsuk.org

Independent Living Helpline
Telephone: 0300 555 1525
Opening hours: Monday & Thursday 9.00 – 13.00
Email: independentliving@disabilityrightsuk.org

ADHD

AADD-UK
Site by and for adults with ADHD

Details: *http://aadduk.org/*

ADDISS:

ADDISS is The National **A**ttention **D**eficit **D**isorder **I**nformation and **S**upport **S**ervice. They provide people-friendly information and resources about Attention Deficit Hyperactivity Disorder to anyone who needs assistance – parents, sufferers, teachers or health professionals.

Details: *http://www.addiss.co.uk/*

Anxiety

Details: *http://www.anxietyuk.org.uk/*
Details: *http://www.social-anxiety.org.uk/*

Autism/Asperger's Syndrome

The National Autistic Society
This organisation provides information, support and pioneering services. The website has plenty of information for students going to university such as:

- A list of colleges for students with Autism or Asperger's Syndrome.
- Advice on choosing and applying for university.
- Starting university – including information on study skills and what to expect.

Details: *http://www.autism.org.uk/*
http://www.autism.org.uk/living-with-autism/
adults-with-autism-or-asperger-syndrome.aspx
http://www.autism.org.uk/about-autism/
research/information-for-pupils-and-students/
autism-information-for-he-students-studying-the-
condition.aspx

Bipolar UK

http://www.bipolaruk.org.uk/

See me

http://www.seemescotland.org.uk/findoutmore/
aboutmentalhealthproblemsandstigma/
bipolar-disorder

Depression

Depression Alliance
The following organisation works to relieve and prevent depression
http://www.depressionalliance.org/

Living life to the full
http://www.llttf.com/

Mind
This gives anyone with a mental health problem somewhere to turn for advice and support
http://www.mind.org.uk/

Sane
http://www.sane.org.uk/

MoodGYM
Games and activities to help individuals with depression
https://moodgym.anu.edu.au/welcome

Dyslexia and Dyscalculia

The British Dyslexia Association
The vision of the British Dyslexia Association is a Dyslexia-friendly society enabling all people with Dyslexia to reach their potential.

Below is a list of some of the online information resources that they provide for students:

- Information for higher education students
- Screening and assessment information
- Books on Dyslexia

Details: *http://www.bdadyslexia.org.uk/*
http://www.bdadyslexia.org.uk/about-dyslexia/
schools-colleges-and-universities/dyscalculia.html

Dyslexia Action
Details: *http://dyslexiaaction.org.uk/*

The Dyslexia Association Ireland
The Dyslexia Association Ireland provides a free information service to the public. Services offered include: psycho-educational assessment of children and adults, group and individual specialised tuition, teachers' courses, summer schools, speakers for schools and parent groups.

Details: *http://www.dyslexia.ie/*

Dyslexia Scotland

Details: *http://www.dyslexiascotland.org.uk/*
http://www.dyslexiascotland.org.uk/adults

Dyspraxia/Developmental Co-ordination Disorder

Dyspraxia Foundation:
The Dyspraxia Foundation supports individuals and families affected by Dyspraxia.

Online resources available from the Dyspraxia Foundation website include:

- Advice for adults.
- Living with Dyspraxia and useful contacts.
- Daily life – coping strategies.

Details: *http://www.dyspraxiafoundation.org.uk/*
Also see www.movementmattersuk.org for more information.

Obsessive Compulsive Disorder

OCD-UK
This site offers information for patients and carers on the condition as well as a location finder service for support groups.

Details: *http://www.ocduk.org/*

Speech, language and communication impairments

AFASIC
Afasic is a UK charity that helps children, young people and their families with the hidden disabilities of speech, language and communication impairments. They have branches across the UK.

Details: *http://www.afasicengland.org.uk/*

RALLI
This is a campaign to raise awareness of language learning impairments and has a wealth of videos and resources.
http://www.youtube.com/user/RALLIcampaign

Royal College of Psychiatrists

http://www.rcpsych.ac.uk/expertadvice/problems/adhdinadults.aspx

Cognitive behavioural therapy
http://www.rcpsych.ac.uk/expertadvice/treatments/cbt.aspx

Tourette's Syndrome

Tourettes Action
Tourettes Action is a charity working to make life better for people with Tourette's Syndrome.

Details: *http://www.tourettes-action.org.uk/*

Other helpful organisations:

National Network of Assessment Centres (NNAC):
NNAC is a UK-wide network of specialist services that work together to facilitate access to education, training, employment and personal development for disabled people. It may be particularly useful for students in higher education as they are often referred to an Assessment Centre for a DSA-funded Study Aids and Strategies Assessment.

Details: *http://www.nnac.org/*

AbilityNet
Abilitynet is a national charity that helps people with a disability to use computers and the Internet by adapting and adjusting their technology. They aim to ensure that whatever your age, health condition, disability or situation you find exactly the right way to adapt or adjust your ICT to make it easier to use.

Details: *http://www.abilitynet.org.uk/*

To be published in March 2014

Amanda Kirby's companion volume to
'How to Succeed in College and University'

HOW TO SUCCEED IN EMPLOYMENT WITH SPECIFIC LEARNING DIFFICULTIES:
A Guide for Employees and Employers

9780285642461   Also available as an ebook

Individuals with specific learning difficulties can often find preparation for entering the workplace difficult while employers can struggle to understand the issues, as well as the strengths, these individuals will bring. In this guide, Amada Kirby outlines how employers can work with potential employees to enhance the workplace and their business.

Includes recommended free apps and software

From advice on how to prepare for an interview, meeting new people and creating a successful work-life balance to the employer's responsibilities under the Equality Act and the training employees may need to work to their full potential *How to Succeed in Employment* is an easy to use and practical handbook based on Amada Kirby's decades of professional, and personal, research and experience.

What are Specific Learning Difficulties?
Preparing for the workplace.
Finding a job and the support available to help.
Interviews.
In the job, etiquette and dealing with others.
Organising your time at work.
How technology can help.
Getting organised at home and looking after yourself.
Socialising – in and out of work.
Mental health and wellbeing.
Guidance for the employer – the Equality Act and building best practice policy.
Useful organisations that can help.

Specifically designed to be dyslexic friendly

Also available in ebook

Dyspraxia:
Developmental Co-ordination Disorder

Dr Amanda Kirby

Dyspraxia is a condition that causes co-ordination problems. It is a hidden handicap, the children who suffer from it look the same as their friends but are dismissed as 'clumsy' rather than treated as children coping with a learning difficulty. Dyspraxia can often go undiagnosed until adulthood and is often mistaken for other conditions, such as autism, dyslexia or attention deficit disorder. In this practical and authoritative book Amanda Kirby asks the questions that parents would like answered, gives a comprehensive outline of what dyspraxia is and how it can affect a child and offers practical advice on how to help a child overcome this problem through-out their life from pre-school to adulthood.

"Dr Kirby's practical experiences and observations of children and adults with dyspraxia is highly accessible and readable, successfully dealing with a very complex subject."

'Dyslexia Contact'

What parents need most of all is information – information about causes, symptoms and other possible conditions, practical ways to improve your child's condition and how to help them to live independently as adults. This book will fulfil the need for relevant information for parents and teachers, medical professionals and play leaders, in a concise, readable and comprehensive way.

"The first wide-ranging and popular guide for parents and others who wrestle daily with the difficulties... It is both immensely practical and written from the heart."

'Daily Telegraph'

Also available in ebook

Down Syndrome:

An Introduction for Parents and Carers

Cliff Cunningham

Professor Cunningham has long been accepted as the UK's foremost authority on Down syndrome and in this third edition of *Down Syndrome* he provides practical, updated, sympathetic and comprehensive answers to every question that any parent or carer of a child with Down syndrome may ask.

"A seminal book . . . The most important aspect is its sympathetic and understanding approach when considering the reactions and feelings that parents may have and how the family adapt and cope."

Down Syndrome Association

Building on the largest survey of children with Down syndrome ever carried out, a survey that has followed nearly 200 children for over 30 years into adulthood, Cliff Cunningham provides accurate, up-to-date and unbiased information that will allow any parent to become an expert on Down syndrome and take informed decisions that are often made about (but not by) the children and their families. Of equal importance are the personal stories provided by parents, which Professor Cunningham includes, for they convey the feelings and emotions that all parents will go through and which they can share with each other.

"A definitive introduction for parents with little or no knowledge of *Down's syndrome* . . . For the uninitiated, Down Syndrome is a good place to start, providing a comprehensive introduction . . . answers thoroughly, but also in an engaging, sensitive way."

'Viewpoint'

Also available in ebook

The Gift of Dyslexia:
Why some of the world's brightest people can't read and how they can learn

Ronal D. Davis

Like other dyslexics, Ronald Davis had unusual gifts of creativity and imagination, but couldn't function probably at school and it wasn't until he was an adult that he discovered techniques that allowed him to read easily. Written from personal experience of dyslexia, this breakthrough book offers unique insights into the learning problems and stigmas faced by those with the condition, and provides the author's own tried and tested techniques for overcoming and correcting it.

"At last! A book about dyslexic thinking by one who is dyslexic, and for fellow dyslexic people . . . I would recommend this book to any dyslexic and non-dyslexic person. It is a dyslexic friendly book."

'Dyslexic Contact'

The experience of being dyslexic is fully explained, from its early development to how it becomes gradually entrenched as a child comes to rely on non-verbal perception. Setting out practical step-by-step techniques, using visualisation and multisensory learning, Ronald Davis brings help to the 15% of children and adults who struggle with reading and writing because of dyslexia. In this revised and expanded edition of his classic work Ronald Davis brings real help to people who have dyslexia.

"Presented in a dyslexia friendly style . . . I would recommend this book, both for people with dyslexia and parents and teachers. It describes the problems so well, but even more importantly it radiates optimism and encouragement."

'Disability Now'

Also available in ebook

Parenting A Child with Special Needs:
Living With and Loving a Disabled Child

edited by Bernadette Thomas,
Cindy Dowling & Neil Nicoll

What is the actual experience of parents who live with and love children with special needs? After the initial shock of becoming a parent, now complicated by being the parent of a child with special needs, as well as having only a confused idea of what may lie ahead how do they find a way forward, to start to build a relationship with their child?

The stories that emerge from *Parenting A Child with Special Needs* are of great passion and, sometimes, pain and, above all, the courageous dedication needed to bring up a disabled child. The editors, Bernadette Thomas and Cindy Dowling, are parents of disabled children who write with real and practical insight into bringing up a disabled child and the relationship it creates. While Neil Nicoll gives a professional perspective into the issues raised.

Parents often come to see their children as a "gift", and the dominant note struck is of the intensity of the relationships that develop between these parents and their children, relationships that are the most fulfilling part of both their lives. They tell it as it is, the joy and the pain, and these are stories that all parents will recognise.